FIRST EDITION

A BEGINNER'S GUIDE TO COLLEGE SUCCESS

JONATHAN GOLDING, PHILIPP KRAEMER, AND DAVID ROYSE

cognella® | ACADEMIC PUBLISHING

Bassim Hamadeh, CEO and Publisher
Leah Sheets, Associate Editor
Christian Berk, Associate Production Editor
Jess Estrella, Senior Graphic Designer
Alexa Lucido, Licensing Coordinator
Joyce Lue, Interior Designer
Natalie Piccotti, Senior Marketing Manager
Kassie Graves, Vice President of Editorial
Jamie Giganti, Director of Academic Publishing

Cover image copyright © Depositphotos/Rawpixel.

Printed in the United States of America.

ISBN: 978-1-5165-1953-8 (pbk) / 978-1-5165-1954-5 (br)

cognella® | ACADEMIC PUBLISHING

We dedicate this book to all of our past and current students who have taught us so much, and to all future students who will walk in their paths.

BRIEF CONTENTS

PREFACE

The three authors of this book have not only been university faculty for more decades than we want to admit, we also have all raised children who have gone to college and been successful. We have seen mistakes that students made and been delighted by their diligence and achievements. After a trial run of some of the content in this book in a computer course free and open to all, we became convinced that we had something important to offer to new, incoming college students—as well as those contemplating college.

Once a student makes the decision to go to college, or at least, begins to consider the possibility in a serious way, questions often arise about how college might be different from high school. Students might wonder how much more difficult college is than high school. If at-home finances are tight, students might have questions about whether they can work part-time while attending college. Adults going to college for the first time may worry about how their various responsibilities may affect their time management.

Indeed, many basic questions arise during the decision process and later when selecting and deciding on the particular program with the best fit. Here are examples of some questions that the *Beginners' Guide to College Success* book poses and answers:

Why should I go to college? What will it do for me?

What is the difference between a college and university?

How do I choose courses to take?

What is a major and how do I pick one?

How much will I be in class?

What is a good balance between studying and other activities?

Will I have time for friends? Will it be easy to make new ones?

Beginners' Guide to College Success has been designed to provide practical advice for students. For instance, it describes different types of exams and discusses tips for studying and preparing for specific types of exams. There are tips on how to get the most from reading (yes, there will be a lot of reading!) as well as advice about how to get maximum benefit from both large lecture classes and small ones. This handy book also recommends getting to know and meeting with instructors, and lists resources available on campus that all students may not know about.

This is a book for parents, too, especially for those who did not go to college. It explains common terms used on campus, for example, *dean, department chair, prerequisite, online courses*. One chapter even discusses the personal freedom that students have when away from home and addresses the personal responsibility they must take for their decisions and lives.

Beginners' Guide provides a breadth of coverage about topics of interest to aspiring college students and their parents. The chapters are crafted to offer quick explanations, suggestions, and tips to guide potential and first-time students wanting take the step up to higher education.

It also lends itself to adoption by instructors teaching *orientation to college* courses for new students. At the end of each chapter are several discussion questions instructors can use to stimulate class discussion or assign to students for reflection papers.

Finally, we want to acknowledge the colleagues and students we work with, and in particular, the generosity they showed by contributing their thoughts and quotes for this text.

ARE YOU READY FOR COLLEGE?

Are you ready for college? Many individuals who are starting college for the first time have heard this question many times. Although you may be sick of it, this question is important to examine. What does being ready mean? Is anyone one really 100% ready for college? College involves a lot more than going to class, studying, and taking exams. You might be ready to take on these three tasks (although you could be a little uncertain), but there is so much more you need to understand about college.

STUDENT VOICES:

I was excited about going to college, but the interesting thing was that there was a moment during my first year that I realized that college was a lot more than I originally thought.

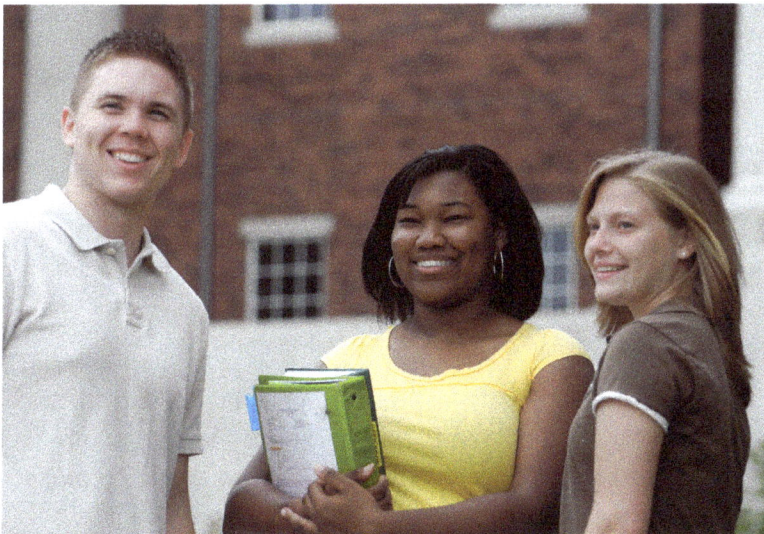

Fig 1.1

WHAT ARE THE DIFFERENCES BETWEEN HIGH SCHOOL AND COLLEGE?

Part of the problem initially is that many students do not think about college as a challenge to their abilities. Like all challenges, college requires the development of a set of special skills in order to overcome the difficulties you will likely encounter. You will discover that college is not simply Grade 13. For a number of reasons, college is not simply a continuation of high school. Let's consider some of the differences.

One difference between high school and college is that not everyone from your high school will be attending your college. There will likely be students from all across the state where your college is located, as well as students from across the United States and from a number of foreign countries. In fact, some of you (especially those attending a private institution) will find that the number of students from your home state is very small because certain schools pride themselves on having a geographically diverse student population.

Second, in general your college courses will be qualitatively different from those you had in high school, with the exception of any Advanced Placement (AP) course you might have completed. However, even considering these AP courses, what you will learn in college is often very different from what you learned in high school courses. A lot of this difference is due to the emphasis on research in most of your college courses. In high school students typically learn a lot of content, but in college there is a focus on the process of discovery— how was that content produced? Bottom line—don't think you know everything about a subject just because you had a class on this subject in high school.

> **STUDENT VOICES:**
>
> *I was scared about the curriculum, but the whole transition part—that was what scared me to death. That is what I focused on, really adjusting to not being in the same situations I had been in for 18 years prior. It was a totally new world. That was the hardest thing to think about.*

Finally, there is the issue of how hard you will be working in college compared to high school. *Hard* in the context of school is a tough word to define, but for now let's just talk about *hard* in terms of the amount of time and effort you must spend on your schoolwork, the degree of difficulty of your courses, and the pace of learning. Over and over again, we hear students say that they did not really work hard in high school. Sadly, we are often told this in the context of a student not doing well on one of our exams, and bemoaning the fact that college exams require a lot more preparation than high school exams required.

The key point to keep in mind right from the start is that the days of not working hard (loafing?) are probably over for most of you. This may not be what you want to hear, but we are trying our best to have you get your head in the game, to understand that your success in college will require you to think about college in a different way than you thought about high school. College requires a lot of hard work, in the sheer amount of time invested, the nature of the work, and how quickly you are expected to learn material.

Unlike when you lived at home during high school, you probably won't have anyone at college encouraging you to stay home and study when you are planning to go to a ballgame or concert with your friends. (Students living with their families could be the exception, of course.) If you invest the time and effort, the end result of this hard work will likely be success in your courses and in moving forward toward your career goals. Success in college includes not only good grades in your courses, but also success outside of the classroom (e.g., making new friends, participating in activities that you never thought about before). We'll talk more about this later.

Fig 1.2

To better grasp the differences in effort required in college and high school, we can provide a way of thinking about how to measure effort. In college it is expected that the majority of work you do for a class will be done outside of class. In fact, most instructors follow an unwritten rule for their courses called the *Three-Hour Rule*. This rule means that for each credit hour of a course you are expected to put in up to three hours of work outside of class. Because it is an unwritten rule, you will not find it written in any college documents, but many instructors still have this expectation. The thinking is that when you are a college student it is your full-time job. Thus, you should be "working" as much as if you had a regular job. So if you were taking 15 credit hours (five courses) during a semester, which is typical at many schools, you would be doing schoolwork for up to 45 hours each week outside of class! Does this mean that every course will lead to three hours of work? Probably not—some courses will require less time and some will require more time. But, we can tell you that on average, the three-hour rule is an important guide to how you should think about your classwork.

Of course, the three-hour rule has big implications if you already have a job or plan to get one. How will this rule affect your time management when you are an adult, nontraditional student who is scrambling to fit in a job and college? In some cases, having a job may require you to take fewer courses than 15 credits your first semester or year. Later, it may not be as much of a problem as you find your stride as a college student. It will be difficult, but with a clear plan and the support of those on campus, you will be able to meet the challenge.

EDUCATION HAS VALUE

You might not be ready for college if you feel burnt out or lack interest in studying. Maybe you have a friend or friends who are taking a year off, sometimes known as a gap year, and you are considering not going right away—or perhaps questioning why go at all.

Just as in high school, you can expect in your first couple of years of college to encounter courses and topics that you have absolutely no interest in studying. Why is this? Why can't you pursue your major right away? Higher education will provide you with a foundation for dealing with a lot of problems and situations later in your career and life. It will stretch your thinking and make your mind more analytical and flexible. It is based on the principle that any and all education is valuable. Here are five ways to think about the value of education:

1. Education increases your knowledge. You will learn facts about the world on subjects ranging from math to art to literature to psychology. More than just learning facts, your education will change the way you think about the world.

> **FACULTY VOICES:**
>
> *I think college is a valuable opportunity to learn how to critically evaluate facts and evidence.*

That is, the knowledge you gain allows you to analyze facts in order to make judgments about something or someone. Think of it this way: you can watch a commercial and be told a bunch of facts about a car. However, it is up to you to take this information and think critically about it in order to decide if you want to buy that car or some other. As you can imagine, too often people just accept the facts that are thrown at them without any real thought.

2. Education prepares you for a fast paced, ever-changing, and unpredictable world. Whether we like it or not, the world is constantly changing. Just think about it—when the authors were your age there were very few computers for public use, no internet, no cable television, and no cell phones—how did we survive? Can you imagine typing a paper on a typewriter and having to use white-out to correct a mistake, or having to have change to use a pay phone to make a phone call (check the web if you don't even know what these are!)? The argument is that as you become more educated, you become more aware of the latest technologies and how these technologies can be used, not only for fun (we all love our cell phones!), but also constructively to deal with the challenges of life. Technology has changed the nature of work.

Fig 1.3

3. Education allows you to gain greater control over your life (what is termed *agency*). In this way, not only does an education allow you to become financially independent, an education also gives you knowledge to think about the world and make your own decisions. In the past, your parents or others may have helped you to make important decisions, but college is the time when you begin to make the tough decisions on your own. As you move through college, you will be taking more and more control of your life.

4. Education benefits society. You are encouraged to share your ideas with others, be it classmates or teachers, and you learn about the importance and responsibility of working with others. In addition, education offers you a chance to become an active member of your community. You can still contribute to society without an education, but as you continue through college and gain critical knowledge, you are better prepared to be a participant (and perhaps a leader!) in the constant changes that society goes through.

5. Education offers you a vast array of opportunities in your life. For example, your education should lead to a fulfilling job and a salary to match. Keep in mind that certain jobs require you to have knowledge from various fields. For example, if you are a lawyer, not only do you need knowledge about laws, but you will be required to communicate with others, both speaking and writing, to understand how people think and behave, and be responsive to those with diverse backgrounds. All of this should make your life have greater meaning, fulfillment and enjoyment—a better quality of life.

WHAT IS THE VALUE OF A COLLEGE EDUCATION?

While high school is important, college increases the value of education even more. You will continue to gain value in your quest for a job and a career. You will not only have more job opportunities, but the data is strong and convincing that college-educated citizens also earn more money than those who did not attend college. For example, the Pew Research Center in a 2014 report found that for full-time workers, college graduates earned about $17,500 per year more than high school graduates. This same report found that college graduates had lower unemployment and poverty rates than high school graduates. All of this points to significant financial rewards if you complete your college degree.

Going back to the point we raised earlier about education impacting society, it should also be mentioned that society benefits as you gain additional years of education by attending college. New engineering graduates will invent new battery technologies, and new ways of traveling with self-driving cars. With a political science degree, new graduates can help craft laws to protect women from domestic abuse. Medical school graduates will develop new ways of treating and helping children afflicted with various diseases around the globe. There are countless ways your college education can work to improve society.

So you can see that your time in college, while an exciting challenge, also has tremendous value and will help you move ahead with a career in an ever-changing world. With this as a backdrop, we are ready to discuss various issues that will put you on the path to success in college.

THE COST OF COLLEGE

You may not be ready to attend college if you have not looked at all of the expenses associated with college. With the yearly in-state tuition at many state colleges approaching the cost of a midsize automobile or more, and more required for out-of-state tuition, the financial commitment is considerable. If your parents are well-off and will fund your education, then you may not need to discuss this issue with them. If, however, they are not willing or able to, this may affect your choice of a college. If you have a strong grade point average (GPA), you should apply for scholarships at multiple schools, foundations, and other sources. If the chances of obtaining a scholarship are low, you might want to discuss going to a state-supported school within your home state versus an out-of-state or private school some distance away. Whether you plan to live in a dorm or in an apartment with other students, it is important to estimate the financial support you will have (e.g., parents, personal savings, and/or scholarships). You may be psychologically ready, but not financially ready for college. Talk to the admissions staff wherever you plan to attend to make sure they know about your financial needs and you know about the costs of attending a specific college.

Some students attend community college, which is considerably less expensive, for their first two years and then transfer to a four-year college or university in their junior year. If you consider going that route, be sure to take courses that will be compatible with the requirements at the four-year institution or you may end up taking extra credit hours at the university to graduate. If you can live at home, you can save money on dorms or an apartment, but you may miss out on some of the social life and independence associated with living at the college. And being ready for college could mean that you take a year to work and save money so that you will not have to rely so much on your parents' support or can borrow less in the way of student loans.

Taking on thousands of dollars of debt to attend college is a really serious matter— especially if the amount needed heads towards six figures. Are you ready to discuss this issue with your parents and university officials? There is no one correct solution to financing college that fits every student and family. You and your loved ones will have to decide what works best for your situation.

QUESTIONS

1. What is your purpose in going to college?

2. What makes you confident that you will be motivated to meet the challenge of college? What are your strengths?

3. What are your career goals?

4. How will you use your current academic skills in college?

FIGURE CREDITS

THE STRUCTURE OF A COLLEGE

How is a college set up (i.e., structured)? Maybe you are thinking this question really isn't very important to you. All you care about is getting into college, getting good grades, and graduating; worrying about how colleges are organized will only hold you back from your college plans. The problem with this way of thinking is that understanding exactly how colleges are structured is extremely important as you navigate the ins and outs of your college experience. In fact, some would argue that without understanding this structure (regardless of whether your college is large or small) you will get off-track, and this may lead you to waste a lot of time and effort getting back on track throughout your college years.

Here's why understanding the structure of a college is important: When you are ready to start something new, it only makes sense that you understand how it functions. For example, if you buy a new cell phone you should know (at least) something about how the phone works. The battery must be charged, you must turn it on, you have to be within range of a cell tower, and so forth. Believe it or not, college is no different. When you are in college, it is critical that you understand how things work on campus. Otherwise, you will join the ranks of other unfocused undergraduates wondering what to do and where to go.

You may now be saying to yourself that if you have any questions about the structure of a college you will just ask friends and relatives. Of course you can do this, and hopefully these individuals can point you in the right direction. The problem is that friends and relatives often do not have the correct answers to certain questions about college. Whoever you ask may not have gone to the same college as you and colleges can differ more than you think. Or, the people you ask may give you an answer that was true when they went to college, but that answer may not be accurate for the way things work now.

With all of this in mind, let's start at the beginning to look at the basic features of how colleges are structured. Consider this: when you go to college, you will have multiple affiliations. You are not just in college, you are part of several different units. First, you become a member of a department that

Fig 2.1

manages your *major*. In college you are encouraged to choose a major—a specialty area of concentrated study. These specialty areas are referred to as *disciplines*. For instance, psychology is a discipline. Other disciplines include English, Hispanic studies, economics, mechanical engineering … we think you get the picture! When you first apply to college or register for classes, you might have already chosen a specific major. Sometimes students decide to have two majors—a *double major*. We'll talk more about choosing a major in just a bit.

Second, everyone ultimately declares a major, but you might also decide (at least at a four-year institution) to *minor* in another discipline. The distinction between a major and a minor is pretty self-explanatory, but just to be clear, you select a major based on what you are most interested in, while a minor is typically a side interest you have or another discipline that complements your major. For example, you might choose to be a psychology major (the study of the human mind and behavior), but minor in sociology (the study of human society, with a specific interest in the changing relationships among individuals and groups). Psychologists and sociologists study different issues, but the disciplines are clearly related—both study human behavior (as does anthropology and even newer fields in the neurosciences). Occasionally, some students select major and minors that appear to be quite different on the surface. For example, students might major in psychology and then minor in Spanish. In the end, your decision to choose majors and minors is up to you. If you can make them work together, or you just are interested in both areas of study, you should go for it!

In addition to being part of a major, you will be part of a group of different majors. Now this can get confusing. Let's start by saying that in higher education we talk about going to a college (e.g., Bates College in Maine, Bluegrass Community and Technical College) or a university (e.g., the University of Michigan, Harvard University). A community college or junior college typically offers associate degrees that you earn in two years, a four-year college typically offers undergraduate (bachelor's) degrees that you usually earn in four years, while a university awards both bachelor's degrees (in four years) and graduate degrees (e.g., master's and/or doctoral degrees). Graduate degrees are earned by attending college beyond your years as an undergraduate—it requires another application process—and can vary in the number of years it takes to earn a degree (e.g., a master's degree can be earned in two years). Typically, universities award more degrees and different types of degrees, and thus usually have larger student bodies than colleges.

In terms of the administration of the college or university, your major will be housed in a department. The level up from your major will likely be called a *division* and it will include related departments. For example, if you are a chemistry major, your professors and you may be in the Division of Natural Sciences. This division could also include biology and physics. The level one up from a division is the college itself. Thus the hierarchy goes:

Major Department $\longrightarrow$ Division $\longrightarrow$ College

Fig 2.2

Now if you are enrolled in a university, things are a bit different. That is, your major department will be housed within one of many colleges. (We know this gets confusing, but the term *college* gets used in all of these different ways.) Examples include a College of Art & Sciences (sometimes called Liberal Arts), College of Engineering, College of Business, College of Education, College of Agriculture, College of Architecture, College of Communications, College of Medicine, College of Law, etcetera. One way of thinking about these colleges is as an assembly of persons interested in the same kind of intellectual pursuits (e.g., engineering, law, business). However, these colleges are still comprised of related departments that manage majors and are often broken down into divisions. For example, a College of Arts and Sciences could contain a Division of Natural Sciences, a Division of Humanities, a Division of Social Sciences, and so on. Here is the hierarchy for a university:

Major Department ⟶ College Division ⟶ College ⟶ University

What is the big deal about knowing how all these pieces are connected? Here's the reason: As a rule, each administrative level usually has its own curriculum requirements. That's right, when you go to a college or a university there are requirements for everything you are a part of. So if you are at a university, you will have departmental requirements (whether it is for a major or minor), college requirements, and then university (usually called general education) requirements. The implications of all of these requirements is that a lot of the classes you take will fulfill specific requirements. Keep three important things in mind about fulfilling all of these requirements: (1) a particular requirement can often be fulfilled by taking one of several courses, (2) some courses can fulfill multiple requirements (i.e. requirements can overlap—they're not all separate), and (3) even with all of the different requirements, you will still be able to take *electives* (i.e., courses not tied to a requirement), which give you additional freedom to choose the courses you want to take.

CHOOSING A MAJOR

With that structural explanation now behind us, let's talk more about majors. It would be nice if some wise person could simply tell you what to major in, but that decision has to be yours (no matter how much your parents think it should be their decision!). For some of you, choosing a major will be relatively easy. Let's say you want to be an accountant. This requires you to major in accounting and most of the courses in your major will be devoted to that topic. This example is what we call a *vocational major* and it involves an applied career you can enter after graduating. Keep in mind that some careers require you to pass certain licensing tests or certifications. For example, most accountants have passed the CPA (Certified Public Accountant) test. Other vocational majors include nursing, education, architecture, engineering, and journalism.

Some of you may have clear professional career goals in other fields. You may be interested in medicine (which could mean becoming a doctor, a physician's assistant, a physical therapist, or other medical professional), dentistry, law, or psychology (as a therapist). You should understand that for these examples, other than psychology, there is not a specific major (e.g., medical doctor) for the careers just listed. If you have one of these career goals you will choose a major in another subject, often directly related to your choice of career. For instance, students interested in medicine, dentistry, or physical therapy may decide to become biology majors. Those interested in law might choose political science or history as a major. After graduating with your undergraduate degree, you would then apply to a specific *professional school* to get a graduate degree. For example, if you want to become a doctor, you will apply to medical schools, and hopefully, four years later obtain an M.D. (medical doctor) graduate degree.

We should add, however, that for these professional fields, the way one thinks about things have changed quite a bit over time. For example, you do not necessarily have to major in a directly related field. In fact, you can major in anything as long as the courses you take meet the requirements of the medical school, dental school, law school, or psychology graduate school you would like to attend. In this regard, we can tell you that there are an ever-increasing number of psychology majors who apply to medical school or law school. The beauty of these changes is that you are no longer constrained to a certain major if you have a particular career goal.

Unlike the examples of specific careers above, it is important to keep in mind that most majors prepare you for a range of job opportunities and professions. For example, if you majored in history, job opportunities include advertising executive, analyst, archivist, broadcaster, campaign worker, consultant, congressional aide, editor, foreign service officer, foundation staffer, information specialist, intelligence agent, journalist, legal assistant, lobbyist, personnel manager, public relations staffer, researcher, and teacher. For many students, having all of these different options is a real advantage; they're just not sure yet what they want to do. However, for some students, not having a specific career path is a big disadvantage. This is because you could end up taking courses that don't meet the requirements of the major you finally decide on. Of course, it will be up to you to determine whether you choose a major that has a specific career path or one that may allow you more options. Luckily, there are many resources to help you get a clear direction on a career—the Internet, career counselors, peers, et cetera. Once you choose a specific major, you will normally have a faculty member or trained staff person to advise you about the courses needed to meet requirements—and also career opportunities with that major.

If you really do not know what to major in, don't become too anxious about it. Even if you start college as an *undeclared*, or *undecided* major, you will be fine for at least two reasons. First, at most four-year colleges, you are not required to declare a major until the end of your sophomore year. Second, it is important that you take the time and effort necessary to make an informed choice. As you take general education requirements (required basic courses) your first year, you will be exposed to faculty who excite you about their fields or point you in other directions.

Exploring different majors requires some research, including reading about different majors, talking to others (students, faculty, advisors), or even taking a course or two in various majors. Other ways to help you decide what to major in are talking to your parents, going to the career center on campus, joining student organizations, and reading campus bulletins and websites. To help you decide on a major and career options, you may be asked (most likely at a career center) to complete an assessment. For example, you make take the *Myers-Briggs Type Indicator* (MBTI®), which assesses personality type to help you think about your interests and preferences for a career. There is also the *Strong Interest Inventory*® that focuses on matching a student's interests in a work environment (and their free time) with education and career goals. Don't be afraid to venture off the beaten path. Most students know what biology and mathematics are generally about, but until you take an anthropology or a geology course, you may not really understand what career possibilities there are in these more "unknown" majors.

STUDENT VOICES:

When I came to college I didn't have my major chosen, and now I would advise people to explore. Say you do know what your major is, still explore different classes. That's what your first two years are for. Then, after your first two years, if you don't like your major you've already found, get out.

FACULTY VOICES:

Shop around! Take a broad assortment of classes and see what is the best fit. Don't be afraid to try out a class that you think you might hate. Make sure that you pick a major that will help you think about the world in a new way.

There are two final points to make about majors. First, feel free to double major. There are times when a double major can serve you well. In some graduate programs or professional schools, you might find a double major to be an advantage. Having a double major in biology and chemistry could help in applying to medical school. Having a second major in a foreign language could be beneficial if you also choose to major in international relations.

There are a few disadvantages that might result from being a double major. These include appearing to be less focused than if you had only one major (particularly if your majors are completely unrelated), and that a double major might lead to a longer time until graduation because of so many required courses to complete. Keep in mind that for

Fig 2.3

some students, it might be best to forgo a double major and opt instead for a major and a minor. You can still show your interests in two domains, but a minor will have fewer required courses to take than another major.

Second, changing your major is not the end of the world. On the one hand, it is okay to change your major because it is critical that you decide on a major that is best for you. In fact, some students will change majors several times before deciding on a good fit. In the first year, many, if not most students, change majors. On the other hand, it is important to understand that when you change majors, you risk delaying your graduation date—the further you are into completing your college credits, the greater the repercussions. This occurs because certain courses you needed for one major are unnecessary for another major, but your new major requires other courses to be taken. Of course, you should check out all requirements for a major and discuss the implications of switching majors with your academic advisor.

QUESTIONS

1. How is your college or university structured?

2. Do you have any idea what you want to major in? What is it and why are you choosing that major?

FIGURE CREDITS

CREDITS, GRADES, & DEGREES

Good teachers always encourage students to regard their education in terms of intrinsic benefits; it is what you learn as a student that matters. True, but extrinsic measures or indicators of what has been learned are also important. Your credentials also matter. College is not just about the experience of learning. The ways in which your learning is measured, validated, and credited is an essential aspect of your higher education. So, let us examine the credentialing process in some detail.

First, it is important to appreciate that a well-organized system exists by which academic credentials are allocated. The end point and primary credential is a *degree*. The specific degree that you earn will depend on your institution (e.g., a two-year community college or four-year university), your specific program of study (e.g., sociology, music, or physics), and the depth study you pursue in that program (e.g., a major, versus a minor or a certificate).

Typically, a degree earned at a two-year college is an associate degree, usually either an associate of arts (AA) or an associate of science (AS) degree. Each associate degree program specifies a set of course requirements linked to some career or area of specialization, such as dental hygiene, civil engineering technology, business administration, liberal arts/general studies, etcetera. The distinction between AA and AS degrees is based on specific course requirements, and those differences are more about tradition than the number of science versus arts courses. Each college or university will have its own distinction between AA and AS degree requirements. One important concept to keep in mind is that completing an associate degree affords an opportunity to transfer more easily into a four-year institution than is possible without completing an AA or AS.

Four-year colleges and universities typically award bachelor's degrees. Similar to associate degrees, bachelor degrees are of two primary kinds: bachelor of arts (BA) and bachelor of science (BS). Again, each institution distinguishes the two types of degrees in terms of specific course requirements. To round out the discussion, some four-year institutions will confer degrees

Fig 3.1

beyond the bachelor degree. For example, there are master's degrees (e.g., MA or MS) and doctoral level degrees (e.g., PhD, MD, EdS). Some teachers at four-year institutions are actually students themselves, working toward a master or doctoral level degree at those same institutions.

The term *curriculum* is a critical concept in higher education, and it is in your best interest to understand the curriculum at your chosen institution in depth. The word refers to the specific collection of educational requirements that must be satisfied in order to earn a degree. The central educational unit for any curriculum is a course (e.g., Introductory Biology, History of Islam, Basic Algebra, Poets of North America). Each course is designed to convey knowledge and develop skills pertinent to the topic of that course. Most courses at colleges and universities are completed within an explicit calendar period (e.g., the fall semester, which may extend from late August to early December, or a summer session, which may last only eight weeks between June and July). Courses might extend for longer or shorter periods as well.

In addition to courses, other curricular requirements are possible. For instance, you may choose a degree program that requires a thesis (a major independent research project), completing an internship, or practical work experience in an applied field, such as education. There are some institutions that also award credit for life experiences outside of school curriculums (e.g., military service).

There are typically three curricular components that satisfy a bachelor's degree. First, you are likely to begin your college experience by completing courses designed to help you develop breadth of knowledge and skills. This curricular component is often referred to as *general education* requirements. Critical thinking, written and oral communication, and quantitative reasoning are standard skill elements of general education. Knowledge elements of general education commonly required for students to complete might include courses in natural sciences, humanities, social sciences, life sciences, and the arts. One quarter to one half of the requirements for a bachelor's degree usually consist of general education courses.

At many four-year institutions, a second, related curriculum component, which extends the general education requirement, is a set of courses required by the university's college that houses your major. For example, a student majoring in political science might be required to complete a set of courses in the natural sciences, humanities, and social sciences specified by a College of Liberal Arts, which might be the administrative home for the Political Science Department.

The last component, the *major*, has become the primary curricular component at most four-year institutions. If you have not already asked yourself, be prepared to answer "What are you majoring in?" As discussed in Chapter 2, each major represents a specialized area of study, often aligned with specific careers or jobs. For example, if you want to be a high school teacher, you might major in secondary education. The major specifies course requirements that introduce you to specific areas of knowledge and skills associated with some focused topic or, as it is often referred to, a *discipline*. Psychology, art history, marketing, electrical engineering are examples of popular majors. In addition to offering a list of required and optional courses, majors commonly restrict the order in which those courses can be taken.

Prerequisites specify courses that must be completed before you can enroll in other courses. Similarly, *co-requisites* specify courses that must be taken at the same time. As an example, if you were to major in mechanical engineering, you would need to have proficiency in math through calculus as a prerequisite for engineering courses. Proficiency might be measured by completing prerequisite math courses or a standardized test. Note that not all courses required for a major are limited to the discipline itself. It is common practice, for instance, for mechanical engineering majors to complete courses not only in math, but in physics and chemistry as well.

Each major outlines its explicit requirements, and it is imperative for you to familiarize yourself with the requirements in order to not only complete appropriate courses but also to do so at the appropriate time. This consideration is especially important for selective majors, which usually require completion of one year or more of prerequisite courses and a GPA minimum before you can officially declare a major.

The term *major* refers to a level of expertise in a particular field based on courses completed, as does the term *minor*. The latter, however, represents a lower level of expertise based on fewer curricular requirements. You might choose to complete a minor that complements your major or broadens credentials to enhance future job prospects. For example, if you were to be a psychology major, you may decide to complete a minor in neuroscience. Similarly, if you major in social work, you may choose sociology as a minor. Computer science majors might also complete a minor in electrical engineering to increase qualifications for specific types of jobs.

In addition to majors and minors, some institutions also feature certificate programs. Certificates frequently require considerably fewer courses than minors do, and often entail specialties that augment a major or a minor by teaching a specific skill. As an example, if you were to major in journalism, you might complete a certificate program in digital literacy. Certificate programs often extend, embellish, or broaden credentials in ways that enhance employment prospects.

Depending on your career goals, it is sometimes valuable to pursue more than one major or minor, and various combinations of majors, minors and certificates are possible. There are two primary objectives to pursuing multiple majors. Curiosity is one motive. You might have multiple interests, and the opportunity to satisfy intellectual breadth is one of the intrinsic joys awaiting you in college. Many students choose to major in two very different areas, such as biology and music, or physics and political science, simply because they have broad interests. The other reasonable motive for pursuing academic diversity is practical benefit; perhaps you will not be able to decide on a single career track, and you want to have two very different career options available when you graduate.

A weaker motive to think very carefully about, however, is to pursue multiple credentials merely to have multiple credentials. Having two or more majors or minors will not always confer a career advantage. The best advice is to seek considerable assistance in making such choices. Advisors, career counselors, faculty, parents, and those already successful in the work world are invaluable resources to guide your academic decisions.

The final curricular component of most four-year colleges and universities is the *elective*. These courses allow you to engage a topic outside the requirements, based on self-interest and curiosity. Usually the course options available as electives include any courses for which there is no prerequisite.

There are two concepts that underpin all curricula and courses: credit hours and grades. Credit hours represent a quantitative measure of your academic progress. It is usually possible to earn between one and four credit hours upon successful completion of a course, although some courses can award more credit hours. The number of credit hours associated with a course depends on the number of hours the course meets each week and the number of weeks the course is scheduled. Many semester-long courses meet for the entire semester, between 12 and 16 weeks depending on the institution; colleges and universities on the quarter system usually meet for fewer weeks during each quarter.

Grades represent a measure of your academic achievement associated with each course. Different grades are awarded based on the level of learning attained as indicated by your performance on tests and assignments. The standard grading practice is to award a letter grade (A, B, C, D, or F) based on the student's performance. Grades other than F, which usually signifies a failing grade, typically indicate that a course has been passed, but some institutions or programs regard a D as a failing grade. Some courses might evaluate your performance simply in terms of pass (*P*) or fail (*F*), or satisfactory (S) versus unsatisfactory (U). It is usually possible to withdraw from a course before it ends, and in those instances the teacher might issue you a grade of withdrawn (W), indicating that you enrolled but did not complete the course.

Sometimes students remain enrolled through the end of a course but cannot complete all of the course requirements due to some extenuating circumstance, such as illness. In these cases, the teacher might issue a grade of incomplete (I), and the student would then receive a letter grade only after completing any remaining course requirements. Usually a teacher and student develop a mutually agreed upon plan for converting a grade of incomplete into a letter grade.

Most institutions record course grades formally in an *academic transcript*. The transcript serves as an official summary of academic progress. It lists grades and credit hours for all courses completed over your college career. The academic transcript also includes a measure that combines letter grades and credit hours. This measure, often referred to as *quality points*, is computed by multiplying the credit hours assigned to a course (e.g., 3.0 or 4.0) by a number associated with the letter grade earned. For instance, many institutions assign a 1 for a D, 2 for a C, 3 for a B, and 4 for an A. Accordingly, for a 4-credit hour course in which you earned an A, you would receive 4 x 4 or 16 quality points. A letter grade of B in such a course would earn 12 quality points, and an A in a course assigned 3.0 credit hours would also earn 12 quality points.

Academic progress is usually summarized on a semester basis on the transcript by calculating a measure called a *grade point average* (GPA). This statistic is calculated by dividing the total quality points earned in a semester by the total number of credit hours completed during that semester. In addition to the semester GPA, your transcript will also include a cumulative GPA, which represents all of the courses you have completed during the entire period of your enrollment at that institution. If you transfer from another college or university, your transcript will include academic credits awarded from that institution. Most colleges and universities have strict rules and policies for deciding which transfer credits to accept and whether grades from those courses are also accepted. That is, some-times transfer credits are accepted but the grades from those courses do not factor in to your GPA at the new institution.

Finally, not all course grades are necessarily included in your GPA. For example, pass/fail grades typically do not affect you GPA, but if passed, such a course might contribute to the total number of credit hours earned. Most degree programs and majors specify the total number of credit hours required to earn a degree (e.g., 120, or 145 credit hours). The total credits required include all curricular components (i.e., general education + major requirements + electives + college-specific requirements).

Each institution establishes its own regulations and policies regarding grading, curric-ular requirements, and granting of degrees. It is imperative, therefore, to explore these policies carefully before enrolling in an institution. Actually, it is reasonable to consider such information when comparing institutions as part of the process of deciding which one to attend.

Fig 3.2

Finally, recognize that your *academic advisor* is an invaluable resource to help you understand all of the academic rules, regulations, and policies pertinent to the issues described above. In addition to providing information, academic advisors can help with registration, class scheduling, deciding whether or not to withdraw from a course, and policies and services available if your GPA falls below acceptable standards. Especially important are the policies regarding academic probation and academic suspension, which differ across institutions. Your advisor will be familiar these policies. Many institutions now provide special intervention programs for students who struggle with academic success and those placed on probation. Some programs even enable students to avoid suspension by completing academic skill development courses. Academic advisors can provide you with the nature and scope of the academic success services available at your institution. Take advantage of these professionals!

QUESTIONS

1. How do credit hours and grades differ as measures of academic performance?

2. Describe the types of curricular requirements included in a bachelor's degree.

3. If you have already chosen a major, why did you make that choice? If you need to choose a major, how will you go about making that decision?

FIGURE CREDITS

Figure 3.1: Olichel, "Graduation Cap and Degree," https://pixabay.com/en/graduation-grads-cap-diploma-907565/.
Figure 3.2: greymatters, "Graduation Caps in Air," https://pixabay.com/en/graduation-teen-high-school-student-995042/.

UNIQUE CHALLENGES

Do you have any challenges that you worry could affect your success in college? Not all students are alike and you may feel disadvantaged, because of some unique factors or issues. These can range from being a first generation student (no one from your family previously went to college), to veterans entering college after serving in the military, to having a disability of some type or special medical needs. In all the examples discussed below, it is important that you realize that regardless of what makes you unique, other students on campus will share a similar characteristic with you. You will not be alone.

To address any fears or concerns you may have about being different from the "typical" college student, there are a number of points you should keep in mind:

1. In almost all cases, there will be people on campus who want to help you. This is so important that it bears stating again: there are offices and people on campus who are there to help. You should never feel that you cannot reach out to others. This is especially true if you are upset with the way you are being treated by an instructor; do not keep everything bottled up inside. For example, if you feel that an instructor is treating you unfairly, start with going to that instructor and talking with him or her. If you are uncomfortable with that, go to the department chair or dean of the college. In most universities, there is also an academic ombudsperson who is an individual authorized by your school to help resolve issues between you and instructors. The ombudsperson will listen to your situation and try to help. If you do nothing, nothing will happen to improve your situation.

2. All students should know their rights, and this may be even more important if you are a member of a minority group. Every college and university will have an office that deals with issues of discrimination based on race, gender, religion, et cetera. It should be easy to find on the website. If you can't find it, go to a faculty member that you feel comfortable discussing the issue with or go to the Dean of Students. Someone in that office will investigate your issues or direct you to the appropriate office on campus.

3. It is best not to limit your friendships only to students who are similar to you. For example, if you are LGBTQ it will probably serve you well to meet with students who are not and to partake in activities with all types of students. College is a time to celebrate diversity, but if you insulate yourself with only those you think you will feel most comfortable with, you will miss making friends with those different from you and won't gain all the benefits of a college experience. Stereotyping of people is not just unfortunate, it is wrong, whether someone from a majority group of individuals on campus comments about someone in the minority, or vice versa. Get to know those in your classes or on your dorm floor who are different from you. They will have knowledge of some things and possibly resources that you may not. Broaden your horizons. Open yourself to learning from the diversity on campus.

4. The college your chose may ultimately not work for you and your unique circumstances. This is often not talked about, but selecting a college is like an experiment. You really do not know the people and the environment there until you spend a significant amount of time on campus. Your choice of a college or university may be great and everything just falls into place. However, it is also possible that your college selection may just not work. Do not be afraid to leave your school and transfer elsewhere. It may take courage to consider transferring to another school, but sometimes that is what is needed in order to move forward and be successful.

Fig 4.1

There are a number of unique challenges students can face during their time in college. We will cover several of these, but keep in mind that there are other challenges that may present themselves unexpectedly. Crises can occur when you or a family member becomes gravely ill. Or, when a parent or source of financial support loses his or her job. There is no need to worry about events like these that come out of the blue. However, there are some more common challenges that many college students face and these will be our focus.

HOMESICKNESS

For those students who live in either a campus dorm or off-campus apartment, life will be very different compared to living at home. The impact of this change can be greater for those who are attending college far from home, but it is a change even if you attend college in the same city where your parents live. Sometimes students who live away from home feel sad because they want to be back in familiar surroundings. Being homesick, at least the first couple of weeks or so, is a pretty normal reaction as students work through an adjustment period in a new location. Some argue that it is important to realize that you are homesick in order to begin working to move forward in your new surroundings.

There are several things you can do to help you with your feelings of homesickness. Most important, stay positive. Give yourself time to adjust and learn your way around the new campus. Explore your new surroundings. Check out not only the campus, but also the city or town it is located in. There's a pretty good chance you will find a great place to study or a cool café to catch a coffee and a snack.

Get out on campus and do things that you like to do. Discover the weight room or the swimming pool, or visit the library. Find a campus organization and join it. This active approach to fitting in on campus could lead to new friends—especially if you invite someone to go with you. Moreover, as you do more things and meet more people you will start to feel at home right where you are.

Thoughts about returning home or even dropping out of college might occur because you feel underprepared for college or are fearing failure, possibly because of doing poorly on an exam or in a course. An abrasive or unfriendly roommate might also make adjusting to college rough for you. But realize that the best antidote to such problems is making friends on campus. Friends can buffer bad situations, affirm that they too did poorly on an exam, and oftentimes can share solutions that worked for them.

Finally, realize that no one is asking you to cut ties to your home. Your friends and family will always be there. Find time to talk to those back home so that you remain connected, but don't do it multiple times every day. One thing to remember is that if you are having problems with homesickness you can always talk to others. You might ask other new students on campus if they get homesick or how they handle their homesickness. The resident advisor in your dorm might be helpful too. If you don't want to talk to your peers about this, all campuses have a counseling office with professionals you can contact.

DISABILITIES

If you are a student with a physical disability, mental disorder, or learning disability, college can be a pretty daunting place. Luckily, there are many ways that you can overcome the challenges of your disability. One guaranteed assistance you have is the law. For example, schools cannot discriminate against you based on your disability (thanks to the Americans with Disabilities Act of 1990). Other laws allow you to receive certain services at college (e.g., reasonable accommodations, like extra time on exams) and technological aids.

> **FACULTY VOICES:**
>
> *No two students with disabilities have exactly the same needs, and no two courses present exactly the same challenges. Students should NEVER depend on instructors to select and implement accessibility solutions for them. Students should ALWAYS meet with their instructors as early as possible, and they must take the lead in proposing and negotiating ways to overcome potential barriers. The student and instructor should expect a course-long partnership that involves a lot of creative problem-solving and a bit of trial and error.*

It is important that you know what resources are available, and to make sure you take advantage of these resources. To find out about these resources, before you get on campus or as soon as you get there, check out the office that deals with disabilities. Make an appointment there and develop a relationship with the staff of this office. In addition, your initial meetings at the disability office should lay out what accommodations you can expect and how they will be offered to you. This includes making sure you understand how to inform instructors about your disability and accommodations. If you have a physical disability, it is also important for you to know the campus. The distance between your scheduled courses, or any buildings without elevators, might be concerns, for instance. The staff in the office providing services to students with disabilities might be able to identify parts of campus that are difficult to travel to because of physical terrain (e.g., steep hills) and to inform you about special parking spaces for those with disabilities. If you believe you have a disability but have never been formally evaluated for it, this office would still be the first place to start for information.

NONTRADITIONAL STUDENTS

Most often people tend to think of college students as recent high school graduates between the ages of 18 and 21, who are financially dependent from their parents and taking classes full time. However, data shows that this description actually fits a minority of students across all college campuses. Today, there are more and more nontraditional students going to college. Nontraditional students are typically over 24 years old, financially independent from their parents, not living on campus, working (part or full time), or may have dependents, in addition to a spouse. For most nontraditional students, taking college classes must be balanced with family and work. This is a lot to deal with and there are only 24 hours in day!

If you are a nontraditional student you will need to set up a study schedule. You simply will not be able to balance everything in your life without a time management plan that takes into account your work hours, family time, class time, and study time. You will also want to make sure that your family understands the importance of your study schedule. Of course, you will have time for them, but they need to allow you to study at those times you have designated in your schedule. You might want to make a practice of studying in the library to avoid interruptions at home, especially if you have small children.

Keep in mind that you can use computer resources to help manage your hectic life. This includes accessing the library, contacting career counselors, advisors and instructors, and communicating with tutors and other learning resources. Your computer is your friend; you just need to use it! Finally, do not feel you need to try and rush through getting your degree. You have enough on your plate. Sure, it is great if you can complete all of your classes in four years, but with a family and other responsibilities, it may take six years or longer to finish because you may need to take fewer courses each semester than a traditional student. Keep in mind, however, that you might also be able to speed up the time to your degree by taking some online classes at home (see Chapter 13 on these courses).

VETERANS

More and more veterans are going to college. If you are a veteran it is important to know that the transition from the armed forces to the college campus is not always easy. One of the biggest issues that arises for veterans is the fact that college schedules are very different than schedules in the military. In college, you have a lot of freedom with regard to your time. You usually can choose classes on the days and times you want, you decide when to study, and you likely will have a car and live off-campus so that you can go and come as you want. This is very different from being in the military, where a regimented schedule is the norm and there is very little, if any choice. Because you will have much more flexibility, it is important that you put some structure in your college life. One way to do this involves setting up a study and work schedule that will allow for a smooth transition. You don't need to have every minute scheduled, but making sure that you know when you have to attend classes and designating specific study times for each class will likely make things easier for you.

Fig 4.2

Another important issue to consider is that the way you think about the world after your time in the military may be very different than your college classmates who aren't veterans. Every veteran will have had different life experiences, and each of you must be mindful that your military responsibilities and the sacrifices you have made have changed you.

Because many veterans are returning to college, there has been a push to offer more resources to veterans. For example, most college campuses have a Veterans Resource Center. This center helps you connect with other veterans facing the same transition, and offers services like tutoring, computer training, and workshops on study skills and writing. Initially, you may prefer to interact primarily with other veterans, and there is nothing wrong with hanging out with peers who you feel comradery with. As you become more integrated into college life, you will likely broaden your contacts to include other students.

COMMUNITY COLLEGE STUDENTS

Community college students can also have challenges associated with transitioning to four-year colleges and universities. Keep in mind that more and more students choose to attend community college. There are many reasons for this, including that some community colleges offer bachelor's degrees in certain areas of study (e.g., nursing), and that community college is a cheaper way to get basic courses out of the way if you want to later attend a four-year school.

The challenges for students enrolling in a community college are very similar to those of students at four-year schools. That is, there are social issues (e.g., making friends, getting involved in campus organizations), financial issues (e.g., loans and scholarships), and academic concerns (e.g., interacting with faculty, study schedules, completing curricular requirements).

However, students attending community college need to deal with a few other issues. Most important in this regard is that community college students must be clear about their long-term educational goals. Do you want to complete your associate's degree and then get a job, or is your plan to attend community college and then transfer to a four-year college or university? If you fall into the latter category, it is very important to plan far ahead. This planning includes determining which four-year school best fits your career goals, and researching policies at potential four-year schools to figure out various transfer policies. For example, will all of your courses from community college transfer to a specific four-year school? You should know that sometimes there are agreements between a community college and a four-year school, which allow for certain courses to transfer and may even guarantee admission to the four-year school if certain criteria are met (e.g., grade point average). Always remember that the internet can be your best friend in obtaining important information about transferring to a four-year school.

To be sure that your long-term plans are on track, make sure to contact an academic advisor at the four-year school you're thinking about attending with your questions—their job is to facilitate transferring to their school. If you plan to transfer, it is important to really work hard to get good grades. Your ability to transfer may depend on a strong record, especially if the program or school you hope to attend has relatively high admission criteria.

STUDENT ATHLETES

A student athlete is a college student who also participates in an organized competitive sport sponsored by their college. The number of such students in the United States is approximately 500,000—a relatively large number. Trying to keep your head together when you have the demands of being a student plus all the demands of a sport can be difficult. The latter also includes various NCAA (National Collegiate Athletic Association) requirements. Although the "student" comes first, there will be times when it doesn't seem that way. How can you deal with these dual demands?

First, be sure to communicate with your instructors about your situation. Make sure your instructors know you are a student-athlete, and that although you will be putting academics first, there will likely be times when you have certain team commitments that you must meet. For example, you may have a road trip for an event or game that conflicts with a course exam. It is almost always the case that your coach or the athletic department will provide a letter for each of your instructors that spells out when you need to miss class. Don't be late with this letter! One thing instructors hate is surprises. Get your letter to your instructors early in the semester so that you and your instructors are on the same page. Also, don't just give the letter to an instructor. Talk to them after class or during office hours to make sure everything is worked out regarding your schedule.

Second, make a plan with someone in each of your classes to help you out with notes and any other information you may miss when you are away at an athletic event. You might even consider setting up or being a part of a study group just to get a bit more support in dealing with classes. Third, it is important that you communicate with your coaches about your academic schedule so that they are aware of your classroom demands. Fourth, as we suggested for other groups of students, it is critical that you develop a study schedule that allows you to manage academics and athletics. Your time will really be constrained, and it is vital that you plan time to get your work done.

Fifth, work with your coach and the athletic department to make sure you will be able to move forward with your career goals. Unfortunately, the vast majority of student-athletes will not find their future careers tied to a sport. (Just think about the small number of individuals drafted to play professional sports by the NFL or NBA each year, out of all of those playing at schools across the country.) You need to make sure you get the proper advice from academic advisors and career counselors to complete your degree (e.g., scheduling classes) over four years and move forward with, perhaps, your potential back-up career plan.

Fig 4.3

QUESTIONS

1. Do you have any unique challenges that you will need to deal with in college?

2. If you do have one or more unique challenges, what is your plan to overcome any obstacles you may face?

3. If you have any unique challenges, do you know whom to contact at your college of choice to help you move forward?

FIGURE CREDITS

Figure 4.1: PublicDomainPictures, "Rainbow Flag," https://pixabay.com/en/rainbow-flag-gay-friendly-13902/.
Figure 4.2: skeeze, "Parachuting," https://pixabay.com/en/parachute-skydiving-parachuting-1416417/.
Figure 4.3: skeeze, "Gymnast," https://pixabay.com/en/gymnastics-female-performance-vault-802990/.

INDIVIDUAL (MY) RESPONSIBILITY

College is a time for taking on new roles and a place where you are authorized to make your own decisions about many different kinds of things. In this chapter, we explore four areas, or decision points, that can impact your college career, and discuss some of the issues associated with decisions connected to them. These decision points are: deciding whether to work, how much and when to engage in social activities, asking instructors for help, and figuring out how to structure free time.

SHOULD I WORK?

We examine this question first from the perspective of adult nontraditional students, then of students with at least one year of college, and finally of those students still in high school.

If you are already employed and attending college part-time or planning to attend full-time but must support yourself or your family, the decision to work or not has probably already been made for you. Instead of deciding whether to work or not, the decision might be whether you can afford to cut back a few hours, say from 40 to 32 hours. Alternatively, the decision might be whether you can find enough time to take more than one course. Sometimes it is difficult for those already employed, or for parents with small children at home to know how many courses to take with their other responsibilities. Fortunately, college advisors are helpful in answering these questions as you discuss specific courses with them. Even if you and your advisor underestimate the time required for the readings, completing assignments, and studying, rest assured that all colleges and universities know that students sometimes have to lighten their course loads. And there is no academic penalty as long as you go through the correct channels to drop your course or courses prior to the deadline posted by the university registrar. If you drop early enough, you may be eligible for a partial refund on your tuition.

If you are a community college student transferring to a four-year program and find it necessary to work in order to remain in college, you probably know the drill. That is, you will likely register for as many hours you think you can manage and then will pay very close attention to the syllabus at the first class meeting. If the course seems too difficult or the instructor a bit rigid about coming in a few minutes late or missing class, you might be inclined to drop the class. If you drop it, you might look around for another section of the course with a different instructor (if the course is required), or perhaps you will go forward with fewer courses if you feel that your remaining courses will keep you busy enough. Some students needing to work decide not to kill themselves by burning the candle at both ends, and are comfortable taking longer to graduate. Other students will tolerate one or two tough semesters in order to push and get done sooner. You have to do what feels right for you. You may benefit, however, from talking it over with those who know you best to see if they agree with the decision you are inclined to make.

There's no hard and fast rule here other than that your college or university might require something like a minimum of 12 credit hours per semester to be considered a full-time student. And if you get loans, you need to be a full-time student. You must be honest with yourself. That is, if you know you come home from your job so tired that you tumble into bed almost right away, then it will be difficult for you to succeed. You may want to take only one course (to go part-time) until you can get your work hours adjusted—especially if the course requires a lot of homework or group meetings with other students.

On the other hand, if you are graduating from high school and going to college, you may realize that you need to work at some point, but you may choose not to do it right away. Not working the first semester can be a good decision. You may need a respite—a period of time to revel in your glorious freedom! Free from parental curfews, stupid school rules, the same old teachers every day! Now that you are on your own (or almost there), college life may allow you to stay up as late as you want, sleep until noon, play video games to your heart's content, and maybe eat pizza for every meal—at least until your funds run low. As your high school years wind down, you may find yourself daydreaming about the free time you will have without the chores that your dad or mom always had ready for you on Saturday, or the sink full of dishes after dinner every night. If you are currently living in a home where your activities are monitored closely (at least in your opinion), or you have been engaged in numerous activities at and after school which have filled up most of your days, you *will* experience college—at least initially—as a breath of fresh air, perhaps even a blast of clean, sweet freedom.

Whether you are a traditional or nontraditional student, the first three or four days at college often are filled with activities. You will learn your way about campus and find places to eat, make any final adjustments to your class schedule, locate the buildings where your classes will be, and attend orientation sessions. You might be asked to volunteer for a community project, and will have opportunities to meet other students in your dormitory, and to attend social activities sponsored by various organizations on campus. There could even be free movies or a stand-up comic scheduled in the student center. Soon though, the calendar will inform you that CLASSES START TOMORROW!

"Wow, that went fast," you will think. And as you go from your first classes to the bookstore, you might be stunned by the cost of the books you will need. Their cost may trigger you to start thinking about the merits of getting a part-time job. As you might expect, there are both advantages and disadvantages to working while being a full-time student.

Fig 5.1

On the plus side, having a steady paycheck can help with expenses and if you have a student loan, it may ultimately mean that you have to borrow less. A part-time job might provide you with the income to date and go to dinner off-campus with friends or attend plays in the city. It could possibly allow you to keep or obtain a car. Over time, you may develop a set of friends at your job—and it is important to have good social support. Another possible advantage is that you might want to keep working for your current employer because he or she has other positions (possibly at higher salary) that interest you or because of the opportunity for a career there. Your employment with that particular employer or company could also look very good on your resume.

On the other hand, employers schedule their employees to work during the hours when they need help. The employer might ask you to work on the afternoon or night before a big exam. You might miss some classes because the employer needs you to come in early or stay late. If you work a full day, you could be too tired to study once you get back to your place. If the job is very stressful, it might prevent you from sleeping through the night or eating properly, which can affect your health. If you are working off-campus and have classes on the same day, you can expect that some days you will be late either because of difficulty finding a parking space or because of public transportation issues. If you are late for class, don't expect a lot of sympathy from the instructor. Instructors usually assume their students are full-time students—or think they should be. And coming in late or missing a class probably is not going to be an excused absence, meaning that it will count against you, even if it's not your fault there wasn't a parking space, that the bus wasn't on time, or that your boss asked you to work late. However, if you are late for class or have to miss it entirely, speak to the instructor or at least send him or her an email to explain your situation. It may make a difference later on when they have to evaluate your attendance or course grade.

> **STUDENT VOICES:**
>
> *I think the biggest things to consider when you're choosing a job, if you have to or if you want to work, is realizing that there are some environments that'll respect that you're a student and there'll be some environments that won't care.*

If you are thinking about getting a job, ask yourself these questions: Do I *really* need the money? Can I possibly get by on my savings and/or parental support? Deciding to work, particularly your first semester, is a decision that requires a lot of thought.

If you *have* to work to support yourself or a family, then at least consider these questions:

- *Can you find work on campus?* Working on campus can save you travel time and expense; supervisors tend to be flexible with the scheduling of hours.

- *Can you find a low-demand job?* Jobs that aren't physically demanding and those in quieter environments (e.g., the library) might allow you to find time to study during your shift.

- *Will you be able to achieve a reasonable balance of school and work?* Falling asleep in class because you had to work too late is a sign that the job is not going to let you succeed in your courses.

Should you work? Each student has to answer this question for him- or herself. If you are sitting on the fence, so to speak, talk it over with someone who knows you well before you commit yourself. And if you do overestimate your ability to juggle classes and work, there is no shame in dropping a course.

FUN WITH FRIENDS (PARTICIPATING IN SOCIAL ACTIVITIES)

You will develop new friends, possibly great friends in college—individuals who may become lifelong friends. Obviously, if you decide to work, you may have less time to develop new friends, although those you work with might become your close friends. Everyone needs and should have friends. In college, you will have many occasions to do fun things with your friends. There will be parties, dances, and concerts, as well as art exhibits, football and basketball games, and so on. You can decide to enjoy life to its fullest at college and, if you want, can probably find students who party almost every night.

In the same way as you must find balance between working and studying, you also must decide how to balance the amount of socializing you plan with the time required to complete things on the academic side—the time you need to read, write papers, and finalize assignments. While it may be that all work and no play makes Jack a dull boy, all play and no academic work makes students fail out of college, or at least to fall below a GPA of 2.0, which could lead to academic suspension. Don't be like the undergraduate in one of my classes who missed a midterm exam but found time to make a Facebook post with a selfie of herself hundreds of miles away in Las Vegas, with a beer in her hand. Absolutely don't make such a poor decision and then go to the instructor two or three days later, asking for permission to take the mid-term exam after everyone else.

Fig 5.2

If you want to have fun with your friends in college, be responsible about it. Look at the dates for tests and assignments in all of your courses. Note these in a calendar of some sort. Refer to the calendar often. If there is some social event occurring the next Saturday evening that you plan to attend, ask yourself if you will have enough time to get all of your homework done on Sunday, or even before Saturday. Be responsible. Plan. Benjamin Franklin reportedly said, "By failing to prepare, you are preparing to fail."

TIME MANAGEMENT: CREATING STRUCTURE

Some students struggle in college because the structure they had in high school no longer exists (e.g., from the parent who woke them every morning, to the set times for athletic practice or study halls). Your new roommate probably won't make a very good parent for you and shake you awake when you oversleep; there are no "study halls" in college, and you have to make decisions about dividing your time between socializing, studying, maybe working, going to class, and sleeping. Further, your old friends and favorite persons to "bounce things off of" are not likely to be around. You may wake up some morning and feel very alone, fully aware that every important decision is yours to make.

In some ways, that is correct. As a nontraditional student, you may have some structure already in place. You may have to drop a child off at day care by 8:00 a.m.; you may need to be at work at a certain time; you may have negotiated with your partner or spouse a block of time on Saturday for studying and writing papers. If you are just coming out of the military, where everything was structured, you may initially struggle with all of your free time. And though you will be older than the typical college student entering as an 18-year-old, you may face some of the same issues discussed below. Squandering valuable time when you should be doing something helpful for your studies can have a negative effect on your college career. Use your time to its best advantage. Manage your time by planning. Make time for those things that are important. In the time left over, kick back, relax, recreate.

As a young adult in college, you will not have the same external structures in place as many of you had in high school. You will have to create your own structure, your own self-discipline. How do you do this? For many students, a good starting place is deciding whether you are a "morning" or "evening" person. That is, do you think best, or more clearly, early in the morning or late at night? This has implications for when you should take classes and when you should study. If you find that things tend to get foggy around midnight, you may be a morning person and should try to go to bed earlier rather than later. If you are a morning person, it is probably easier for you to get up to attend 8:00 a.m. classes. And that might free up your afternoons for doing homework, or at least, allowing you to finish your homework prior to 10:00 pm. If you are a night person, you probably prefer to avoid morning classes, sleep later, and start your homework around 10:00 p.m. It does you no good to start writing a complicated paper for a course if your mind isn't clear. You can bring some structure into your life by deciding how much sleep you need. Are you an 8–9 hours type of person or do you do well with six? Should you go to bed early or doesn't it matter?

STUDENT VOICES:

> *You have to figure out how to manage your time to get your homework in, to focus on what classes need to be studied or material learned—if you have tests or something like that; so I think time is a really big issue, and you need to try to figure out how to fit in school, work, homework, and everything else you're trying to do.*

As we suggested earlier, you can also bring structure into your life by planning, and noting due dates on a calendar. If you just received a phone call from some new friends wanting you to go to a movie Sunday night and you have a paper due early Monday morning, it may not be in your best interest to go. Although it might be difficult to pass up the opportunity, have the internal discipline to recognize that a fun thing might create problems with your grade in a course. You might still decide to go if the paper is a minor one and the movie starts early, but evaluate the possible consequences if you opt for fun rather than completion of your assignment—particularly if you are a morning person. Do not box yourself in by putting off your assignments and projects until the last minute. If you do that, you will not be able to participate in something socially enjoyable that comes up at the last minute—and on most college campuses, something is always happening. You have the most flexibility when you stay current (caught up) with all your assignments.

Knowing when tests will occur and when assignments are due require that you have read your syllabus for each course all the way through. Read the syllabi carefully to note dates when you might be absent because of conflicts with other courses and activities (e.g., a field trip, play rehearsal, recital). Also, there might weekends when you were thinking of leaving campus for a visit home; look to make sure that you have accounted for all of the important dates for all of your courses. Read the syllabus carefully to see what else you might learn. For instance, in courses with a lab component (e.g. chemistry, physics), the syllabus might give an explanation that, although you will conduct experiments with a lab partner, each of you has to write up your lab reports independently. Each year some freshmen fail to read their syllabi and get charged with plagiarism, because after meeting in class, and in an "ignorance is bliss" kind of mode, lab partners wrote one lab paper that they made copies of and turned in separately.

Look for ways you can manage your time effectively. For instance, if you have a two-hour break between classes, perhaps you can find a quiet place to do homework. That could free you up later in the evening to play a game of tennis or hang out with your friends. Prioritize the things that are important to you. Make sure they get on your calendar!

ASKING INSTRUCTORS FOR HELP

A college student recently remarked that he did not understand what was going on in his Calculus III class and was afraid that he might fail the course. When asked if he had met with the instructor during office hours, or if he had even asked for further explanation before or after class, the student replied that he had not. This student, a sophomore with a tremendous grade point average, ignored the advice of other faculty. "Go meet the instructor," they said. "Introduce yourself. Ask the instructor to show you how to solve the problems that you don't understand."

Fig 5.3

Faculty who teach usually encourage and enjoy interactions with students. If you are struggling in a course, turn up your courage a notch and go visit the faculty member during his or her office hours. The instructor may be able to show you ways to approach the problem that you had not considered, to break it down more simply, or might remind you to do something that you have forgotten. Don't let your shyness or hesitancy to speak to a faculty member outside of class force you into a lower grade than you want. Saying this another way, take responsibility for the grades you want!

If you don't understand something, then seek help. Sometimes it is possible to find another student in the class doing better than you who will agree to help you with homework or will study with you for tests. There may be a teaching assistant or a resource on campus that you haven't made use of. Might the internet have a good explanation of the concept? At any rate, do not passively sit in a class when you are sweating the possible end-of-the-semester outcome. Talk to the teacher or your advisor. Make a plan. Take action. Your grades are up to you. Every instructor, at the end of the semester, can point to students who should have asked for help. Don't be one of those. As a nontraditional student, you could possibly be older than your teaching assistant or instructor. Don't let that get in your way of asking for assistance if there is something you don't understand!

QUESTIONS

1. How do you feel about working while you go to college?

2. What are some ways you organize your time?

3. What are some ways to strike a balance between social time and school time?

IMAGE CREDITS

COMMUNICATING WITH PARENTS AND FAMILY MEMBERS WHILE IN COLLEGE

The transition from high school to college entails a dramatic period of change. Both you and your extended family will feel the impact of this transition. While in high school, you had the benefit of the guidance and structure provided by those close to you, including parents, grandparents, older siblings, friends, teachers, counselors, and others who supported you. The college experience represents a profound shift to a very different lifestyle.

You no doubt look forward to this exciting period, but it is also reasonable to have some apprehensions. And it is important to realize that your extended family will experience the change as well but from a very different perspective. If you are a younger student going to college from high school, you will think more about your greater freedom and the chance to manage your own life. Your extended family, in contrast, will be excited for you in watching you assert your independence, but they will also feel some anxiety, a sense of loss, and apprehension as they celebrate your growing maturity. If you are an older,

Fig 6.1

nontraditional student, who may be a parent, you may be more apprehensive about your ability to succeed in school, especially if you have been away from an academic environment for some time. But even nontraditional students may need to manage new relationships with friends and family. How you prepare and manage your changing relationship with your extended family and friends during this critical transition is an important aspect of academic success. If communication with those close to you is ever important, now is one of those crucial times.

Pause for a moment and consider this question: What do you think you and your extended family and close friends should talk about regarding how you will relate to them during your college career? As you ponder that question, we can offer some advice. As you begin your college career, be intentional about your interaction with those who have been close to you. Think in advance about how often you will communicate with them and what you want to share with them regarding your college experience. You should also think about when to seek their help and advice. Independence is a two-way street, however. As you look forward to asserting greater independence, others upon whom you have depended will also *expect you* to actually become independent.

A general principle that seems to work well is for extended family and friends to remain connected and supportive but from a distance. You need some space. You can certainly preserve the positive bonds that have formed over the course of your life while you recalibrate, for example, your student–guardian relationship. To realign a relationship is not to abandon it. The critical implication is that taking responsibility for your academic success does not mean cutting yourself off completely from those who have nurtured and supported you. Your need to accept responsibility for your successes and your failures does not require that you isolate yourself. Rather, it requires establishing expectations that meet your needs as well as the needs of others close to you.

To that end, one issue to resolve concerns the boundaries that you and others significant to you need to establish for how often you communicate. Remember, although those close to you need to adjust to your greater freedom, they will never be free from worrying about you. At one extreme is the student who contacts home after every class, and at the opposite extreme is a student who decides to never contact home all semester. Based on your personal, unique relationship with your guardians you should be able to find a point between these two extremes that respects both parties.

In terms of what you communicate, you again need to contemplate some gentle boundaries. You certainly do not want to isolate yourself from others, but neither should your college experience become a reality show for friends and family. A regular summary of how things are going seems reasonable. Your parents do not need a detailed daily transcript of your life. And do not be overly selective in what you share. There is a tendency for students to communicate the positive and hide the negative. But if you only share your 'A' grades and avoid sharing a quiz that you failed, you might be losing an opportunity to benefit from their support and guidance. Your guardians have more experience with the ups and downs of the world than you. Most adults have experienced both success and failure. Their advice and support can help you overcome academic challenges, especially if you confront failure. You may not realize it, but your guardians can be an invaluable resource for managing your academic achievement.

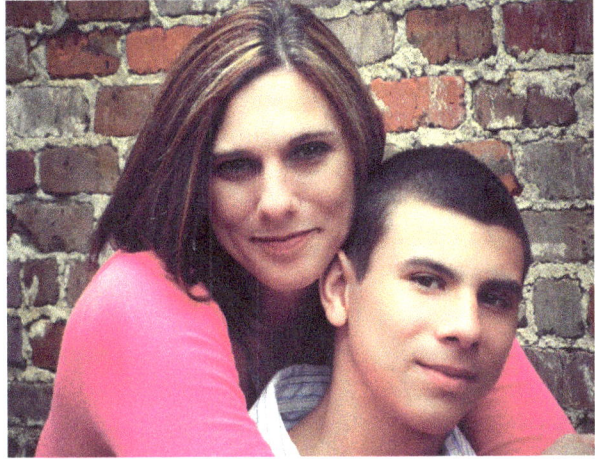

Fig 6.2

PARENT VOICES (TO OTHER PARENTS):

However hard, resist the urge to call professors or other college officials regarding absences, grades, or homework assignments on behalf of your children: Always let them learn how to handle such issues on their own.

One of the saddest situations is a student misleading those who care about them. Do not be the student who lets friends and extended family assume that they are excelling in college until the end of the semester, when grade reports reveal that you are on academic suspension. It is not unreasonable to experience some academic difficulty in college, and those close to you can be a good source of advice and motivational support. Do not shut them out!

In a sense, your relationships with others involve partnerships. Parents, siblings, grandparents, spouses, close friends, and even coworkers are more than willing to help you. The challenge is to establish levels of support that enable you to take responsibility for your academic success without depending too much on others. There are times that you might need to be assertive with your support network; those conversations may be difficult, but in the end these kinds of discussions contribute to your overall development. Do not be afraid to talk!

Finally, as you begin to traverse the college landscape, it is worth reflecting on the fact that other people important in your life have devoted themselves to preparing you for success. Students do not excel in college without a strong foundation, and many people have invested in you. As you begin to reap the benefits of a strong foundation, reach out to those who have helped prepare you for success. One of the most rewarding calls a parent, a sibling, a friend, or a former teacher can receive is from a college student who calls simply to say, "Thanks for all that you have done for me."

QUESTIONS

1. How do you think communication with your parents will change?

2. What advantages do you see to being more independent in college?

3. What worries you most about being more independent in college?

FIGURE CREDITS

Figure 6.1: fabiennefrancis, "Family," https://pixabay.com/en/family-portrait-smiling-people-1888619/.
Figure 6.2: Greyerbaby, "Mother and Son," https://pixabay.com/en/mother-son-people-family-hug-58987/.

ATTENDING CLASS

Should you attend class? This question only applies to students in face-to-face-classes; we will discuss how attendance applies to online courses later. The question about class attendance is both interesting and complicated given that most colleges do not have a universal attendance policy. That is, many of the instructors in your college classes will leave it up to you whether to attend or not, with the unstated assumption that you are still responsible for anything that actually goes on in the classroom. Think about how different this is from high school, where your teachers were constantly charting who was or was not in class, and where an attendance clerk was the rule not the exception.

Despite the fact that some students decide not to attend class often, we advise **you to attend all of your classes**. Some students argue that it is not worth going to class. We have heard all of the reasons for not going. These include: 1) the class is ridiculously boring, 2) it is a large class where no one would even know if you were present or not, 3) not much learning is occurring even if class is attended, 4) there's too much other work to complete for other classes, 5) "I can read everything in the book.", and 6) PowerPoint™ slides are posted or videotapes are available. For us, as long-time educators, it is sad to hear students say that being in the classroom is not worth their time. Of course, we cannot change their instructors or how they deal with their classes, but we still feel strongly that there is always something of value going on in the classroom. Moreover, while you might have an instructor who does not take their teaching seriously or is generally not good in the classroom, we feel that the benefits of attending class outweigh the costs.

So why should you attend class? We think there are several reasons to make the effort to get to class. Keep in mind that these reasons will only matter if you actually go to class and pay attention the entire time. If you go to class, but end up frequently consulting your phone or looking at eBay on your laptop, you might as well not have attended. First, class time can be interesting and fun. For example, it is one thing to talk about the brain, but to be shown an actual brain in class is pretty cool—you can't get this when you're sitting in the dorm playing Pokémon. Think about learning a foreign language. Yes, you can learn Spanish by watching a video, taking an online course, or reading a book written in Spanish. The key is that the experience of attending class and being an active participant in your learning (i.e., actually talking to others in Spanish) far exceeds the experience of passively watching a video or reading a textbook.

Fig 7.1

Going a step further, keep in mind that when you are in class you are offered the instructor's perspective (and even that of other students) on the course material that will enhance your learning experience. Instructors often add personal experiences or *war stories* about their experiences as students or researchers that help make the material come alive. Also, you have the opportunity to ask questions in real time if you are confused about the course material. Instructors can add helpful hints about learning, offer simpler explanations, and even express disagreement with textbook authors. In these ways, the classroom opens up a vast array of possibilities for learning, and your instructors (if they are worth their pay) will constantly work to make you feel as though you never want to miss class. Through discussions, demonstrations, and lectures, instructors should motivate you to show up and be eager to learn. (OK, maybe eager is too strong for some students, but at least *receptive* to learning.) Although we can't promise that every class will be a wonderful theatrical production, most faculty work hard to provide you with the essentials of what you need to master the content and in that way, to make your class experience something to look forward to. We should add that your classmates may also offer insights into the class material, over and above that of your instructor, as they ask questions and share life experiences. This, of course, can lead to class discussions that really get you to think critically about material, and to make connections that you could never make if you were just sitting in front of your computer. To us, going to class and enjoying the diversity of thought and experiences is what college is all about.

STUDENT VOICES:

I pay for school. I see it as it I'm losing my money if I don't show up to class.

Second, attending class often impacts your grade. That is, more and more instructors are giving students an incentive for coming to class by tying an attendance policy to the evaluation criteria of the class; attending class and performing in-class activities earns points toward your final grade. The activities might include writing answers to in-class questions, or using clickers (classroom response systems) to answer questions raised in class. With regard to the latter, clickers are basically a way to have audience participation. Your instructor may ask the class a multiple-choice, yes/no or true/false question, and students click on a small electronic device (sometimes you can just use your cellphone) to answer. The interesting aspects about these clickers is that they are tied into a computer data base and when you respond you get credit for that response. In this way, the instructor can keep track of who was attending class when a certain question was asked, as well as how well students understand the material. We should note that in-class assignments are typically worth from 5–10% of your grade, so just going to class and completing the assigned in-class activities increases your overall grade.

Third, another way to bump up your grade by attending class has to do with the correspondence between lecture and exams; questions on exams often come directly from lectures. In today's college course, it is a rare class that takes all questions directly from the book. Some students skip lecture and simply get the notes from a classmate. However, hearing the lectures in person often far improves your ability to learn the material than getting notes from a lecture you did not attend. (Think about not being able to attend the first showing of a movie you wanted to attend but a friend offered to take notes for you. What would you miss by not being there in person?) Keep in mind that getting notes from a classmate is not as simple as it seems, at least with regard to actually learning from the notes. For example, your classmate almost surely takes notes in a different way from you. They can leave out important information that you would have included, and add a lot of notes that you might think are irrelevant. In addition, the time it takes your classmate to go over the notes (if they are even willing to do that) or to get them to you might be longer than the time it would have taken you to just attend the class. You also should consider that if your friend's notes are taken in longhand, you might not be able to read them easily.

Fig 7.2

Fourth, research has found a positive correlation between class attendance and class performance; higher attendance leads to higher grades. This body of research includes a study by one of us. Golding (2011) conducted an archival study of 5,150 students across an 11-year period (1998–2008) from a large Introduction to Psychology course at the University of Kentucky. The classes over the years were similar in size (437–505 students per class), were each taught during the Fall semester at the same time of day, on the same day, in the same room, and by the same instructor (the author of this article), and had four 50-question exams during each course covering almost identical topics and using similar questions. Golding found a highly significant positive correlation between attendance and exam performance for each class. While a correlation does not indicate that attendance was the cause of improved grades, there are also experimental studies that showed attendance improves performance in a more causal fashion. In those studies, undergraduates took the same course, but some classes had an attendance policy and some had no attendance policy. The experiment showed that for classes with an attendance policy, grades were higher than for classes with no such policy.

FACULTY VOICES:

Every semester, I tell students that class is like life, where success only happens for those who show up. That means to be successful in the class—and even more importantly, to learn something in the class—they have to be, physically present, as well as mentally present.

A fifth reason for attending class moves away from learning and grades. Instead, this reason focuses on the social impact of being in class with your peers and the instructor. Every time you step into a classroom you are given the opportunity to participate in one of the joys of college—interacting with others. When you go to class, you are no longer an isolated college student, you are part of a community. With this community comes the ability to talk to other students and hopefully make new friends that can last a lifetime. Who knows, you might even meet your future partner in class!

As far as your instructors, remember that they can lead to big dividends as you move through college and into your career. For example, you might need a letter of recommendation for a job or graduate school. These letters take time to write and strong positive letters aren't guaranteed—especially if the instructor doesn't recognize you or know anything about you. Getting an instructor to write you the kind of impactful letter that can help you in the future could well start with your classroom attendance. By being in class and talking to your instructor, the two of you will know each other at a deeper level, leading to not only a great letter, but also a relationship that goes well beyond a grade in the course. Moreover, your attendance will show the instructor that you are highly motivated, a trait that goes a long way when presented in a letter of recommendation.

The sixth reason you should attend class is that going to class pays dividends when it is time to study for exams. It is likely that your time in class will make material clearer, mostly due to the instructor clarifying issues and explaining things in a way that you just can't get when you are by yourself. Because being in class helps you understand the material better, you will cut down on your actual study time. Another important aspect of being in class is that instructors often make comments during class that guide you when studying for an exam.

Lastly, not all college instructors round up the final grade average. For instance, you might see that your final grade is 89.47, which might result in getting a "B" in a course, or an "A" if rounded up. In our experience, instructors are much more likely to round a grade up if they recognize the student's name because he or she participated in class and had good attendance. While no student plans to be on the cusp between two grades, it is not uncommon.

For all the reasons we cited above, we believe that you will find enormous benefits from attending class. Will there be some days that you wish you had just stayed in bed? Of course! But, in the long run, we feel very confident that attending class on a regular basis increases knowledge of the course material and will greatly enhance your college experience.

QUESTIONS

1. What kinds of things can you do to motivate yourself to attend class?

2. Do you plan to take classes at certain times of the day or certain days in order to help you attend class?

3. When you attend class, do you have a plan for how you are going to interact with others in the class, including the instructor?

FIGURE CREDITS

Figure 7.1: dschap, "Classroom," https://pixabay.com/en/classroom-computer-technology-1189988/.
Figure 7.2: claude_star, "Classroom With Some Empty Seats," https://pixabay.com/en/convention-conference-meeting-1410870/.

TALKING WITH AND INTERACTING WITH FACULTY

In high school, you spend a LOT of time with your teachers. The good ones may help you to develop an interest in their subject. They may inspire and perhaps encourage you to think of yourself as someone who could succeed in college. The bad ones may drone on and on, give you tons of busywork to keep the noise level down in class, and give the impression that they seldom have a clue about anything. Whatever their strengths or weaknesses, you share the same classroom with them for almost a year and become almost as familiar with them as a family member. In college, however, your exposure to teachers (we call them professors or faculty) is considerably briefer. The standard course meets for three hours a week and even part of that time you may be doing something online or in a lab with a teaching assistant. The faculty member may or may not grade your papers; depending on the size of the class, a teaching assistant may grade them. And often your exposure to an individual faculty member only lasts 15 weeks (one semester), unless the faculty member teaches multiple courses in your major. So you may know much less about any individual college faculty member than you knew about your high school teachers. The other side of the coin is that they also know very little about you. This might present a problem.

Imagine you are in the library one Sunday evening with a group of students who tend to hang out together. As you are working on a paper for Monday's English class, you get a phone call and you leave your laptop to step out of the study room to take the call. While you are out, one of the other students in the room suffering from writers' block takes a look at how you opened your paper in order to get started himself. All goes well with the call. You come back, finish your paper, and submit it the next morning. Three days later, you receive an email from the faculty member accusing you and the other student of plagiarism. It turns out the other student "borrowed" your opening paragraph, stating it verbatim in his paper. The instructor's problem is that he can't tell who wrote the original paragraph and who copied it. The instructor doesn't know you and doesn't know that you would never do anything so stupid! Given your limited exposure to faculty in the classroom, what can you do to let your instructors know who you are and to learn something about them?

LEARNING ABOUT FACULTY ROLES AND RESPONSIBILITIES

Let's start with what you might want to know about faculty, no matter whether you attend a two-year or four-year college, a private, or a public one. There are levels of accomplishment (academic ranks) for instructors within higher education. At the lowest level are teaching assistants, who are students themselves, but generally graduate students working on a PhD degree. Working under the supervision of a faculty member, a teaching assistant may be your laboratory instructor, the individual who teaches your course, the one who grades your assignments, or a recitation leader when a section of a large lecture class meets separately. If you want to make conversation with teaching assistants or get to know them better, ask about the research they conduct or hope to conduct on their way to finishing their degree.

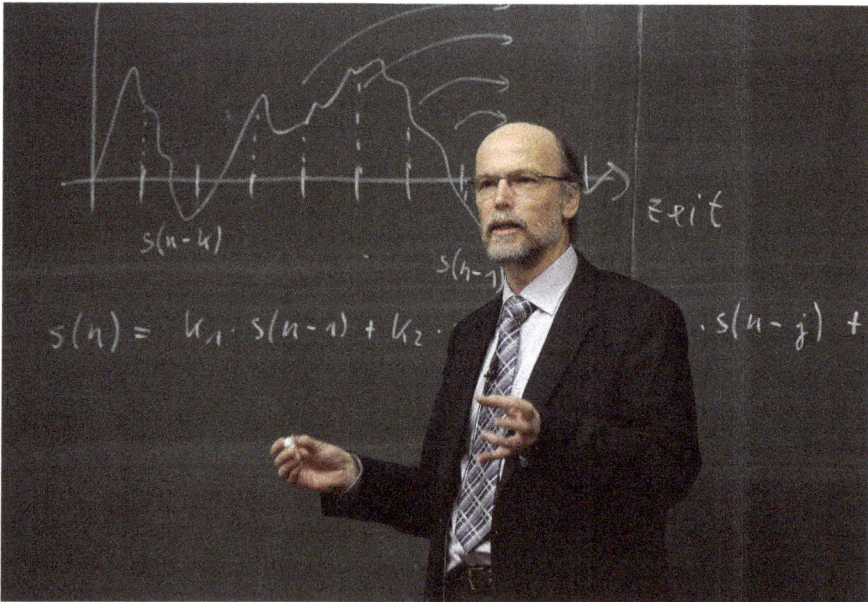

Fig 8.1

Part-time faculty, also known as adjunct faculty, are also fairly low on the totem pole even though they may have a master's degree or even a PhD. They tend to be hired for one or sometimes two courses per term. Part-time faculty could be recent graduates of a program or those who may have some special expertise or knowledge (e.g., a child mental health therapist). An emeritus professor might also teach part-time. That title means the person has formally retired but has been asked to come back and teach a course, possibly because another instructor is not available for that particular semester.

Full-time faculty (along with administrators) are the ones who decide upon the curriculum you must follow and make policy decisions like the criteria for admission, and so forth. The academic ranks for the full-time faculty consist of four main groupings. Assistant professors are usually the newest faculty members. They often have just acquired a PhD in the last four or five years and do not have tenure. What is tenure? Tenure is when the faculty of a program and the administrators of the college or university value the contributions of the faculty member and want to keep that person around. Tenure means that the faculty member is considered permanent at the institution unless there is some unforeseen crisis like a major budgetary cutback or some extreme violation of school policy. Tenure is based on an individual's accomplishments; it is not a popularity contest. Assistant professors may not get promoted or tenured if their faculty colleagues do not feel that his or her teaching and scholarship are valuable, significant, or sufficient. Unfortunately, part-time or adjunct faculty members do not receive tenure. To get to know adjunct professors better, ask them about their undergraduate experience or what they do when they are not teaching. You may be surprised by where else they are employed or by their research interests—besides teaching students!

The next level up from assistant professor is associate professor. This distinction means the faculty member has obtained tenure and is able to chair important committees, like dissertation committees for students working on their PhDs. Above the associate professors are the professors (sometimes designated as full professors). These individuals have achievements (like a national or international reputation) over and beyond the associate professors. Once a faculty member becomes an associate professor or professor, he or she may have opportunities to move into the administration of the college of university. For instance, the Dean is usually a full professor who is responsible for oversight of a college and its day-to-day administration (e.g., seeing that bills and salaries are paid, representing the college in meetings and functions, and so forth).

You may not always know whether the faculty member teaching your course is an assistant, associate, or full professor (you can usually find this information on the school's website). However, it is always okay to refer to him or her as "Professor" or "Dr." That title shows respects and most faculty expect it. Do not call faculty members by their first name unless they tell you that is their preference.

When your instructor is not in the classroom, what is he or she doing? Full-time faculty have interesting jobs that may involve efforts in three or four categories. We'll start with teaching since this is likely the role you see first. Teaching is more than delivering the lecture or posting PowerPoint slides on the computer. It may take an instructor three or four hours of reading, finding resources, and preparing for every 50 minutes of lecture that you experience. Then, once back in the office, he or she may need to advise students, meet potential new students, grade papers, or start getting ready for another class.

Fig 8.2

The proportion of time that a faculty member devotes to teaching depends on several factors. In community colleges and smaller colleges, faculty may spend the vast majority of their time teaching and advising. However, in large universities, faculty members may spend less time teaching and approximately 40% to 50% of their time devoted to research. They are engaged in planning studies, gathering data, analyzing it, or writing reports about their research. Some faculty members are essentially full-time researchers and teach just occasionally. However, there are a lot of individual differences within programs and colleges. Some faculty decide to become administrators of programs (such as being the director of an undergraduate or graduate program) and their duties keep them from teaching full-time.

Faculty in the larger schools also are expected to provide service to the community, state, or nation, and to their college, university, and profession. At the local level, this might mean serving as an expert or board member for some agency or public school, advising some group in the state's capital, or serving in an elected office in a national organization (e.g., American Psychological Association or National Association of Social Workers). Colleges and universities have numerous committees and most faculty serve on several, such as committees focused on admissions, curriculum, promotion and tenure, budget, and committees that arise when new faculty have to be hired or special events planned. In addition to all their work responsibilities, faculty members may have families, children, or aging parents to care for, and are in many ways, just like any other family you know. Their diverse and varied responsibilities often explain why they are not always in their offices.

Community college faculty tend to teach more courses per semester than their colleagues at research universities and so you might find them in their offices, in between classes. Part-time faculty often have separate day jobs and may teach only in late afternoons or evenings.

Most faculty whether new or old, full-time or part-time, at the community college level or research university, will feel comfortable talking about why they have chosen to be an educator. They will be happy to talk about their hobbies, books they are reading, and vacations they have taken or plan to take. They may even show you pictures of family members. If you are considering going from a community college to a four-year school, or wondering about the best graduate school, another great topic for conversation is schools or programs you should consider. Ask career advice, ask about the best and worst aspects of careers. It is also always safe to ask any questions about their research, or specific assignments, what you are learning in their classes, or something that you are still struggling to understand. Although we've said it before, faculty really don't mind such questions.

College faculty also differ from high school teachers in that their perspective on teaching can be very different. They expect *you* to take responsibility for what you learn. Their role is to guide you. In this role, they will expand your knowledge but want you to become a critical thinker—one who doesn't just accept information but who is able to evaluate it objectively. They will appreciate your curiosity and questions about their subject matter.

Most faculty, with few exceptions, actually enjoy helping students learn. They don't mind and actually enjoy conversations with their students. You should not fear faculty. If they have posted office hours, drop by and visit them at least once. Or, make an appointment with them by email. You'll be surprised that some faculty may actually remember your name—even in a large lecture class. If you use email, be respectful in this way: refer to Dr. Jones or Professor Smith. Don't say "Hey, can you see me next week?" Instead, write: "Professor Anderson, would you be available to meet with me next Friday at 2:00 p.m. after class?" Sign your name in case your email address doesn't make it clear. (I [Royse] once had "goobergirl" send me an email.)

Even if you are in an online or hybrid class, you can still reach out to faculty members by email or phone or Skype or Zoom. Many have virtual office hours. Follow up on something by emailing, "Dear Professor Smith, I was really interested in our reading last week about the electron microscope being able to see the movement of proteins into the nucleus. Could you suggest another reading about the movement where I could learn more about all the things that proteins do within a cell? And also, will I ever get a chance to see something like that myself? Do you have any videos or photographs you could share with the class?" Later, you might want to send another email and perhaps the two of you could have coffee or meet sometime when you could ask other questions about the preparation needed to have a career in the field, availability of scholarships, and so forth.

Why should you get to know faculty members better? There are many reasons. Let's say that you want to apply for a job or a scholarship and need a faculty member to write a letter of reference. You would want to ask the person who knows you best. Who would that be?

STUDENT VOICES:

Every lecture I had I went to my teacher's office.

FACULTY VOICES:

Don't be afraid to go to office hours! Faculty set aside that time to meet with students and are typically happy to have students come by. It is a great way to introduce yourself, ask questions, and build a relationship with a faculty member that can help you in the future when you might be looking for internship opportunities or recommendation letters.

Fig 8.3

A professor in your major area may know of opportunities within the department or may even have a research project that needs assistance, such as someone to collect or enter data into the computer. Even if the faculty member does not have funds to pay you, the project could be in your area of interest and could lead to a larger role in a research project later, or even an appointment in a few years as a graduate assistant or teaching assistant. Sometimes you can register for an independent study course, and volunteering to help with a research project can earn college credit.

More practically, suppose it is the end of the semester and you end up with an overall average of 89.49 or 89.56 in a course. Do you think you deserve an A? Well, some faculty don't round up and the policy is stated in the syllabus. However, if you are on the borderline between passing and not passing and the faculty member knows you by name and you have good attendance, you have a better chance of receiving a passing grade than if the faculty member doesn't know what you look like or who you are.

While it is not likely that a faculty member will become your best buddy, most are friendly. Some will even have coffee with you—and buy! Your take-away from all this is that there is no reason to be intimidated by faculty—and we cannot think of a single reason why you should avoid introducing yourself or meeting your instructors.

So now you know something about how the faculty are organized and how they spend their time. How do you start a conversation? You can ask, "What other classes do you teach?" Or even better, "What is your favorite class to teach?" If the instructor has mentioned something in class about his or her research, ask about that. Is it a primary interest? Why? How long has he or she been engaged in this particular research project? Ask about an article or paper where the faculty member has reported his/her findings. What journal would it be in and how do you find it? Questions like this will get you started, and at some point, the instructor will ask about you: where you came to the school from, your hobbies or interests, what you are thinking about in the way of a career, and so on. It won't be difficult, we promise!

QUESTIONS

1. What things did you learn about talking with faculty from this chapter that you did not know already?

2. What are your thoughts on tenure? Good thing? Bad thing?

3. What can you do to prepare to meet and interact with faculty?

FIGURE CREDITS

Figure 8.1: WikimediaImages, "Man Professor Lecturing," https://pixabay.com/en/birger-kollmeier-professor-910261/.
Figure 8.2: jsoto, "Woman Professor," https://pixabay.com/en/woman-office-teacher-613309/.
Figure 8.3: tiyowprastyo, "Man Professor," https://pixabay.com/en/teacher-lecturer-writer-counselor-99741/.

GETTING TO KNOW OTHER STUDENTS: WHY BOTHER?

No man is an island, entire of itself; every man is a piece of the continent, a part of the main. If a clod be washed away by the sea, Europe is the less, as well as if a promontory were, as well as if a manor of thy friend's or of thine own were; any man's death diminishes me, because I am involved in mankind, and therefore never send to know for whom the bells tolls; it tolls for thee. (John Donne, [1624], *Devotions Upon Emergent Occasions, and Severall Steps in my Sicknes*)

When you arrive on campus to begin your college career, you may have friends from high school or your hometown also attending the same college or university. Don't be surprised, however, if you don't run into them frequently. College officials often make it a practice to encourage the development of new friendships and social encounters by placing individuals from the same high school or locale in different dorms, if possible—or on a different floor at a minimum. Usually, although there may be exceptions, your new roommate will be someone from a different part of the country, someone you've never met before.

Why? One of the fundamental, but unstated, goals of a college experience is to broaden students' horizons. This should not only be a goal of your college or university, but should also be your personal goal. That is, not only should you become aware of different perspectives and cultures and ways of viewing the world, but you should also try to gain an appreciation of the rich diversity of the humanity that inhabits our planet. If you are from rural Illinois, you might find that your roommate is from Los Angles; if you are from Philadelphia, your roommate could be from Florida. As you talk with each other that first day or two, you may discover that you have a great deal in common, or you might find that you have nothing in common except that you are sharing the same room or suite. Friendships can and do develop despite differences in backgrounds, families, majors, and so forth. As you talk together, you may find that you both like the same music, enjoy athletics, or have the same hobbies.

STUDENT VOICES:

I was the only person from my high school who came here, so I had to make friends. So I forced myself to make friends.

The college administrators who oversee the dormitories on campus know how important it is to facilitate interaction among residents within dorms. Even after orientation week when special efforts are made to help residents meet residents, there will be activities and opportunities for socializing. In many dorms, resident advisors do schedule activities like movie nights and trivia contests where residents can have fun and make connections. Why is this important? Because these events and activities allow you to meet and get to know those living in your dorm that you would otherwise just walk past in the hall or stairway.

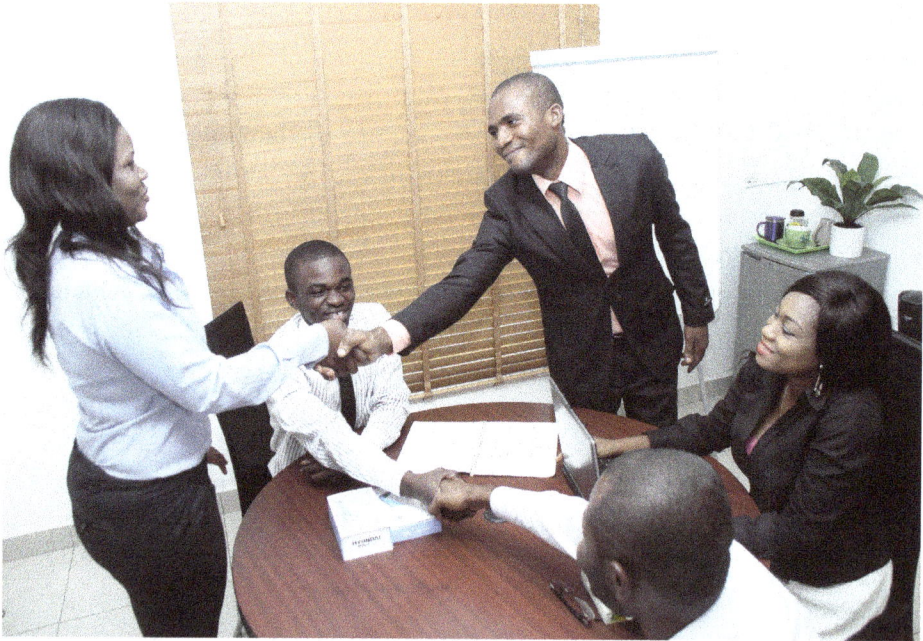

Fig 9.1

My first year in college, I (Royse) quickly bonded with someone I never would have encountered in high school. Coming from a small rural farming community, I was scared that my educational background wasn't strong enough to succeed in college. In several of my classes another freshman, a young man whose family came from Puerto Rico and who grew up in New York City's Spanish Harlem, similarly wanted to do well in his courses, but also felt anxious about his ability to get good grades. Before every major exam, Josh and I developed exams for each other to test what we had been studying and learning. To cut the story short, we both did well academically. After our undergraduate degrees, he obtained his law degree and I got my PhD. And by the way, he and I are still friends!

Another fellow that I met later on as an undergraduate told me about a great job where I lived rent-free off-campus my last two years. I would have missed a wonderful opportunity had I not struck up a conversation with him.

How do you meet other students? You start by saying, "Hello." If you are on your way to the bus stop, in your dorm, in the gym, in the bookstore, or so many other places on campus, and the face is familiar, you might say something like, "Aren't you in the Monday morning physics section with me?" You don't have to know the other person's name to talk to them. Extend your hand and say, "I'm Sarah," (or whatever your name happens to be). It is highly likely that the other person will then give you his or her name. Conversation can then proceed. One of you might ask the other person if he or she had had difficulty completing the last assignment. And who knows? The two of you might agree to meet to tackle the next assignment or to study together.

You should not feel that you can only approach people to whom you have been introduced or met in class. There is no law that says you cannot talk to someone you have never met before. For example, you might be in the mood for some exercise. If you see someone from your dorm or apartment building who seems friendly, consider inviting them to go with you. Even if you don't know anyone, you can still go to the basketball courts and you should feel that it is OK to ask if you can play. Having experienced this in my college career (Golding), the answer is almost always "yes." Not only do you get to play, but there is a high likelihood that you can come back another day and the same players will be there. Keep playing and the chance is also high that you will develop a friendship with one or more of the players. Maybe you'll be invited to go along with a group to get something to eat afterwards.

A chance meeting like those described above is one thing, but remember you will be sitting around classmates in each of your courses. Even if Sleepy, Grumpy, Sneezy, and Dopey are sitting in the four seats around you, they won't be sitting beside you in every course. If they are, simply change your seat and see if you can make a connection with other students in your class. Conversing with students to your left and right is a great way to make new friends since you already have something in common (the course). Related to being in class with other students, another good way to get to know other students better is to form a study group. What often happens is that the study group can morph into social gatherings that have nothing to do with your class. Study groups are a great way to develop friendships whether you are a recent high school graduate or a nontraditional student.

STUDENT VOICES:

You get to know the people around you and you talk about the class and you talk about other things and sometimes you make really good friends, friendships that last a really long time.

FACULTY VOICES:

I encourage students to introduce themselves to students who sit around them. Students usually sit in the same seats every day and it is an easy way to build a quick class network. I encourage them to exchange contact info with each other. Those classmates can be helpful if you are confused about something that happened in class, miss class notes, or simply want to commiserate.

Fig 9.2

Keep in mind as you think about talking to someone on campus that everyone is pretty much in the same boat as you. Everyone is looking to make friends because human beings are social creatures. However, they could also be anxious about talking to others who they may not know. If you smile and notice others around you, don't have earbuds buried deep in your ears, or your cell phone held defensively 12-inches from your face, you will find that other students will want to talk to you. The student sitting next to you may notice that you did really well on the last quiz and might initiate conversation to ask you for help in the course. There will be multiple opportunities to make close friends and acquaintances with whom you share a particular goal (e.g., to survive the Calculus course). The key point here is that college is not the time to fade into the background and become invisible. Be confident, walk forward, and talk to others!

Making new friends on campus is not being disloyal to your old high school friends—or even a boyfriend or a girlfriend. While you may have plans to move back to your hometown after you graduate, in the meantime you need another community, your college community, to support you emotionally and psychologically, and to be fully integrated into college life. It is simply more fun to have friends to go to the ballgame with than sitting alone in your room, more fun to go to see a movie or attend any campus activity with a friend or two than it is to go alone. You need a community of friends at college, and here's the good news: You can be a citizen of more than one community! It is possible to have friends at home as well as at school.

In addition to meeting peers in the dorms and in your classes, clubs and organizations on campus provide a fun way of meeting students. Usually there is a central directory of these organizations and many have offices in a central location (like the Student Center) so you can walk there and talk to someone. Make the time to investigate some activity that has always held your interest. At our university, the Student Organizations and Activities webpage shows 32 clubs listed under Hobbies/Interests, ranging from caving, chess, and building a solar car to yoga. The category of Service/Volunteer has another 48 organizations, including groups that build schools in Honduras, train service dogs, provide a camp experience for children whose parents have cancer, and there is even a Random Acts of Kindness Club. Additionally, there are 52 Departmental, 62 Professional, 18 Recreational, and 37 Religious/Spiritual organizations registered as student organizations. In addition to all of these activities are the sororities and fraternities on campus. For some students, getting involved in the Greek system is a great way to meet your peers, and it allows you to be involved in an organization that participates in social activities, philanthropic pursuits, and often intramural (within the university) athletics. But you can also find intramural sports and co-ed sports without joining a fraternity or sorority. On most college campuses, there seems to be some kind of organization for just about everyone. Quite frankly, it seems pretty likely that you can find some organization that captures your interest—if you look.

Nontraditional students may not have the same interest in socializing with younger students. That's understood. There may still be organizations on campus to support vets, single parents, and other groups. Further, if you wish to learn more about you area of study or have a special interest, you can ask faculty members if you can volunteer to assist with their work. You may find that you could be introduced to, and become friends with, graduate assistants and teaching assistants who are closer to you in age.

> **STUDENT VOICES:**
>
> *The more you're involved in, the more you're going to make friends.*

C. S. Lewis wrote, "Friendship is born at that moment when one person says to another: 'What! You too? I thought I was the only one.'" Whether you feel lost on a large campus, homesick, uncertain whether to buy an expensive reference book, or disappointed in a grade, having other students as friends can brighten your day and give you a different outlook. That's the value of getting to know other students! Make friends! Get involved in campus life!

QUESTIONS

1. Who is in your community at college? (Or who do you think will compose your community?)

2. Do you make new friends easily?

3. What would help you to feel more comfortable when meeting new people?

FIGURE CREDITS

Figure 9.1: adabara, "Students Shaking Hands," https://pixabay.com/en/colleagues-seminar-presentation-437024/.
Figure 9.2: dcondrey, "Students at Table," https://pixabay.com/en/students-group-university-school-1084597/.

TAKING COURSES: WHAT DO I REALLY NEED TO KNOW?

WILL COURSES BE DIFFERENT FROM HIGH SCHOOL?

Yes, they will be different. You were hoping I would say this, weren't you? College courses will, for the most part, be very different than the majority of those that you took in high school—with the possible exception of AP courses. How will they be different? In high school there is usually a lot of time on task working at your desk. In college, however, the first thing you may notice is that each class is primarily centered on a lecture. The instructor may or may not have you working in class at all, depending on the subject. Most of the time, you will be scrambling to write down or type the key points that the instructor is making. Yes, there will be homework or assignments to help you master the material, but you will usually do these outside of class, on your own time. This will especially be true in large lecture classes.

CHOOSING COURSES TO TAKE

Another way that your educational experience will be different from high school is that you will have so many choices to make. While there will still be general education requirements and requirements for your college and major, even within those three divisions you will have choices. For instance, for a humanities course you might choose between courses on Greek and Roman Mythology, Introduction to Music, Introduction to Women's Literature, German Film, or Major Black Writers, among many others. For a science course, you might choose from the Solar System, Introduction to Physics, Chemistry I, Environmental Geology, or Genetics and Society, to name just a few. In the social sciences area, you might select from Anthropology, Archaeology, Communications, Psychology, Public Health, Sociology, and still others.

How do you choose between them? The first level of decision has to do with your educational goals—if you already have some in mind. You might be handed a sheet at orientation that tells you exactly what courses you should take to be an electrical engineer. As a psychology major you could decide to

Fig 10.1

enroll in Intro to Psychology your first semester. Or, perhaps you note that your psych major requires Intro to Sociology. You could take the sociology course to meet the requirements or jump into your psychology course your first semester.

Perhaps you are unsure what you want to do or what major to choose. Generally, that's not a problem because the college or university's general education course requirements are so broad that almost everyone can find something of interest. For instance, have you always wondered how archaeologists pull details from bone, pottery, and shreds of fabric to understand a culture that existed hundreds or thousands of years ago? Have you been eager to take your first computer science class?

A second level of decision has to do with when the courses are offered. With the general education, or core courses, there are likely multiple sections of the course. In college, most courses fit either a Tuesday, Thursday meeting schedule, or a Monday, Wednesday, and Friday schedule. The classes for courses that meet three times a week generally meet for a shorter time (e.g., 50 minutes) and those that meet twice a week meet slightly longer (e.g., 75 minutes). Usually there are 10 minutes between classes. Students who need to work often try to create schedules with most of their courses on Tuesdays and Thursdays.

In colleges that use the semester as an academic term, you will generally take five courses that are three credits (or three hours) each. If you pass all of your courses at the end of the semester, you would have 15 credit hours. Generally, it is not a good idea to take more than 15 credit hours your first semester unless you have excellent self-discipline and study skills and won't be working. Although, taking 16 credit hours by adding a one-credit course for something like ballroom dancing or archery could be fine.

The bad news about being a first year student is that all of the other students who were at your college last year have likely registered before you; some of them needed the same course as you (say, Archaeology) and might have already taken all of the seats, or perhaps only a few seats remain open. Those seats go to the students who register for them first. Don't forget to register for classes and don't wait until the very last minute. But if this happens, you will likely discover that most college students avoid the 8:00 a.m. classes, so there could be seats left in courses that meet at that time of day. Meeting twice a week is more popular than three times a week (because it leaves more days open), so the twice a week sections of courses often close first.

If you need to work during the day, you might gravitate towards evening classes. Some of these may have a different meeting pattern than the day classes. For instance, you might find evening classes that meet once a week, but for three hours for each meeting. Depending on your work schedule and other responsibilities, you may also decide to take online courses. The online course pros and cons are discussed in Chapter 13 (Distance Learning).

Another feature that you should note is that the large enrollment courses could have a lecture on the first day of their weekly meeting (e.g., Tuesday) with the next meeting that week being a lab section, or discussion section—sometimes called a recitation. Or, you might have a lecture each class meeting. Other courses have two lectures a week plus an associated lab or recitation day each week. A recitation section is where several small groups have been created from the larger lecture class. Teaching assistants (usually graduate students) generally conduct recitation sections, and their job is to encourage questions, clarify content, and create discussion about the lecture. The teaching assistant might also provide in-class exercises to help students self-assess and determine if they understand the content. As you develop your class schedule, pay attention to both the time and day of the lecture, and also to the days and times the associated lab, recitation, or discussion section meets, if there is one.

Note that student loans or financial aid packages might require you to register for a certain number of courses. That is, you may not qualify, in some instances, if you drop down to part-time status and take too few courses. The college's financial aid office can help you navigate this issue.

FINDING "GOOD" COURSES AND INSTRUCTORS

The good news (which might also remind you of our advice to talk to other students) is that sophomores and juniors can often recommend instructors they have liked and those that they didn't. However, instructors can get reputations that may not always be fair—especially when they are teaching required courses that students didn't want to take in the first place. Instructors can also be judged to be "hard" when they expect their students to study and take the course more seriously than faculty in the other sections. You may discover that not every faculty member is a great teacher. An undergraduate told one of the authors not long ago about an instructor of a large lecture class who never made eye contact with his students. The instructor stayed focused on the whiteboard or looked off to the side—even when answering questions. Information like this may help you choose which section of a course to register for.

Besides information from friends, your college might post student course evaluations that you can consult. Your advisor or another faculty member may be willing to be candid about some great professors for you to take class with and maybe even discuss the lesser luminaries. There are also websites such as ratemyprofessor.com, which often contain some evaluative information about individual instructors. The only caution here is not to pay a lot of attention to any website (e.g., www.ratemyprofessor.com) that contains only a handful of evaluations of a professor. Students who are upset or bitter about a grade can blast professors, and you would have no idea whether that comment was representative of all the students; it may even have been completely fabricated.

Your instructors will be college graduates with somewhere between three and five years of graduate education on top of that. While you may encounter some instructors who only have a Master's degree, they may be working towards finishing their PhD degree. The vast majority of your instructors will already have a PhD. As explained in Chapter 8 (Interacting with Faculty), your instructor will have many other responsibilities besides teaching the class you sit in. Some faculty see themselves primarily as researchers and that is their passion. For them, teaching occasionally may be something that they either don't particularly enjoy or don't take the time to do well because of other obligations. Other faculty, including some researchers, will be superenthusiastic about their subject matter. Most faculty take their teaching responsibilities very seriously, try to do a really good job, and hope you will, too.

Sometimes when you have the freedom to choose a course, you may not know anyone who can tell you the "inside scoop" on the course or its instructor. Even the official brief course description might not give you enough information to let you know whether it is too technical or advanced for you. Generally, courses for first year students have lower course numbers or identifiers (e.g. PSY 100) than courses for juniors and seniors (SOC 435). While that might be a tiny bit of help, you may want to try and obtain a copy of the syllabus to see what the course covers. A copy of the syllabus may be posted electronically by the department or exist somewhere within university's webpages. If you can't find it there, you might call the department office to see they can provide you with a copy. And if none of that works, then you can also contact the faculty member directly to see what the course requires.

The syllabus is a document that is like a contract. It outlines what you as a student have to do to succeed in the course. It should provide a week-by-week outline of the required readings and assignments, explain how your grade will be determined in terms of how much each assignment or project counts, and the grading scale. There should be contact information for the instructor, resources (e.g., supplemental readings), and instructions for completing each of the assignments. As a rule, instructors usually hand out or post syllabi electronically by the first meeting of each class.

In large lecture classes, you can generally expect presentations with PowerPoint slides. Some faculty will post these electronically for you to download before or after class. However, some faculty do not do make them available outside of the classroom. The issue here is the ownership of intellectual property that the instructor created. He or she may not want to see the slides posted on the internet. With this in mind, you should always find someone in each of your classes that you can ask for notes and any other information about class in case you need to miss a lecture.

Although instructors can create educational materials from many different sources, if a textbook is required, you will be expected to rent or buy it. Further, you will be expected to actually read it. Do not think you should be able to do well in a class by just studying the PowerPoint slides. Yes, textbooks are expensive but they are part of your education. If you can't afford to rent or buy the text for a course, see if one of your classmates will go in half with you and the two of you can share. Also, check if your instructor will put a copy "on reserve" at the library that you can borrow for a few hours or a day. Finally, you might also want to check at the library to see if there is a copy you could check out for a longer period of time. Know that it is your responsibility to keep up with the readings. It is not the instructor's job to nag you to read or remind you twice each class meeting what the readings are for next week.

ELECTIVES

Smaller classes are often available as electives and almost every major allows you to choose some non-required elective courses. Generally, you take electives after finishing the general education requirements—that is, during your junior and senior year. However, sometimes when all the courses a first year student needs are already full, the student is advised to look for an elective to take. Unlike the large enrollment classes where there is a mixture of students from many different majors, in the smaller elective courses you may find that most of the students in an elective course have the same major and most are very enthusiastic about the class. This might be because they are passionate about being poets and want to learn to write better poetry, or because they want to visit the Mayan ruins at Chichen Itza and want to learn more about that culture. However, this generalization isn't always true.

Fig 10.2

Students in a beginning photography class may have many different majors but share a desire to improve their photography.

Electives are generally considered fun courses and you should investigate new topics by looking into the college's elective offerings in different departments. Particularly if you haven't decided upon a future career or major yet, explore courses (whether large en-rollment or small) that you think might interest you. College advisors can very likely give you some advice if you are completely befuddled about what you want to do with your life. And most colleges have a counseling and testing center where further guidance and standardized aptitude tests are available.

In most colleges electives have a pass/fail option, which means that you can take the course without it affecting your grade point average. This is great news if you want to take an elective like Chinese or photography but feel a little apprehensive about how well you will do. The pass/fail option also means that you may not have to do all of the coursework or worry about exams in the way that students taking it for a letter grade do—not that we endorse skipping assignments. If the course is not thought to be all that difficult, then you might actually want to register for it as a graded course because a high grade could help improve your GPA. Pass/fail courses count for credit only and appear on your transcript. However, instructors may not know that you are taking the course pass/fail until recording grades at the end of the semester unless you mention it to them.

Another option is to register to audit a course. This means that you simply sit in to listen to the lectures, read the readings (if you have time), and participate in class discussions. Generally, little is required of you, but you should discuss with the instructor his or her expectations about how much you will need to do. Note that you will get no credit for the class but if will show as an audit on your transcript. However, there are no implications for your GPA.

Both auditing a course and taking one pass/fail are good ways to explore a topic that you are interested in but know nothing about.

QUESTIONS

1. If you have decided on a college or university you want to attend, have you investigated the course-meeting pattern? How will its meeting pattern affect you if you have to work while a student?

2. How will you keep track of the various assignments and responsibilities in your courses? Will you use a notebook, an electronic calendar? Do you usually need to be reminded of due dates?

3. Have you thought about courses you would like to take the first semester, if possible? If so, what would you choose?

4. What do you think is the most important consideration in deciding what classes to take in college? What would be the least important consideration?

FIGURE CREDITS

Figure 10.1: TeroVesalainen, "University Sign," https://pixabay.com/en/university-education-school-2119707/.
Figure 10.2: WikimediaImages, "Minority Student in Class," https://pixabay.com/en/anishia-davis-woman-female-person-876169/.

SUCCEEDING IN LARGE LECTURE CLASSES

In college, for better or worse, many of you will likely encounter large classes. In case you're wondering what *large* means, it's relative; that is, the size of a particular class is defined in comparison to the size of the other classes at your school. At a big university you might have 30,000 total students on campus and large classes of several hundred or even close to a thousand students. Your class might have more students than your entire high school graduating class, and this can be pretty daunting to think about. Do NOT let this overwhelm you!

If you think that any big class is bad and should be avoided, you need to change your thinking, because it's simply not true. Moreover, if you hear a student say that a large class was *bad*, it's hard to know what that means. It could mean the content was difficult, that it was boring, or that it was about a subject that the student had no interest in, but had to take because the class was required. Keep in mind that some of the best classes you will take may be large classes and some of your worst classes will be small classes.

One of the most important factors that determines whether a large class is successful is the instructor; there are countless examples of students packing a lecture hall just to hear a certain professor teach. Most instructors who teach these classes are volunteers, because teaching this kind of class requires a lot of work. Instructors not only have to make sure that each lecture is highly organized, but also have to be prepared to deal with many more students than normal. They generally have to be more organized than other instructors because the class would be unmanageable if they weren't. Therefore, your instructor will know how to speak clearly, present demonstrations, show videos, and use other technology (e.g., social media) with the class. The key is that an experienced and motivated instructor will work hard to make a large class more like a small class.

Instructors who teach large classes often have a certain personality. It is hard to pin down that personality, but one way to think about it is that great instructors of large classes really show (verbally and nonverbally) how much they love being in front of a crowd. In addition, these great instructors always think of exciting things to do in class that motivate students to attend. These

Fig 11.1

include exciting in-class demonstrations and group work where you get to interact with your classmates. In addition, instructors are starting to take greater advantage of the power of social media with their large classes. For example, they may use sites like Facebook and Twitter to allow a large class to gain a greater sense of community. These sites allow students to communicate with each other about class issues (obtaining notes, clarifying questions, posting comments and information about study groups, etc.) on a 24/7 basis. The key is that an experienced and motivated instructor will work hard to make a large class cohesive. You'll feel part of a community, rather than feeling like an isolated student. One last thing to keep in mind is if you get into a large class and you can tell right away that the instructor just doesn't care about the class (let alone you), it probably is just best to drop the class, move on, and add some other class.

When you take a large class, it is all well and good to have an energetic instructor. However, your success in a large class depends a lot on you. That is, you have a big responsibility in a large class—possibly more than when your class is much smaller. So what can you do to help yourself survive in a large class? Here are some tips that we think will help you out when you take large classes. First, avoid any temptation to get lost in the crowd. With so many students in the room, it is very easy to lose yourself in the crowd and become anonymous, to lose your individuality. Some of you might like the idea of fading into the background with so many other students in the class. We would argue that this would be a BIG mistake and really take away from your college experience, and probably impact your grade in a negative way—lack of interest usually leads to less motivation, which leads to less studying, which leads to lower grades. Be yourself, not a number!

FACULTY VOICES:

Be very organized and disciplined. Most instructors design survival into their courses provided you stay on top of deadlines and basic expectations.

Second, it is critical that you make your best effort to attend class! Don't think that no one will care or even notice that you are missing if you don't attend a large class. This may be true in some large classes. However, more and more instructors of large classes are using teaching techniques that are graded and that serve to promote attendance. These include in-class writing assignments and "clickers". The latter are devices synchronized with a computer that allows an instructor to ask questions and get student responses in real time via clickers. If you fail to attend class, you will get a score of 0 on these assignments and thus lower your grade in the class. For those who want to argue that these kinds of in-class assignments do not really reflect your grade, please remember that instructors are free to include various graded components as part of your overall grade. If you do not feel you will be able to make the effort to attend every class, you should not enroll in the class. As a final point about the importance of attending class, keep in mind (as we discussed Chapter 7) that part of the college experience is being in the classroom, interacting with your instructors and with the other students in class.

FACULTY VOICES:

I would say that to survive a large lecture class you need to attend all of the classes and recitation sessions. The reason you are in college is to learn the material in your classes and the best way to do that is to actually attend the classes. The lectures will reinforce the ideas that are presented in your textbooks and your professors are very good at stressing the really important components of all of the material covered during the semester.

Third, try your best to get to class early. When you get to class before the class begins, you give yourself a better chance to get a seat near the front of class where you have a great chance to talk to the instructor. Also, you have some time to talk to the people who sit near you. It is important to get to know people in your class, not only for notes (in case you get sick and miss a class) but because your classmates are potential life-long friends. Finally, you might ask why it is important to get a seat close to the front of class. Not only do you give yourself a better chance to talk with your instructor, but it forces you to be more focused on the lecture. That is, instead of looking around the room at everyone to see what they are doing, when you sit near the front all that you can see is the instructor and the screen.

> **STUDENT VOICES:**
>
> *Sit toward the front. The professor sees you. Plus, if you have a question, then they call on you, everyone is in back of you, you don't even see them. It's less distracting.*

Fig 11.2

Students often ask us if they should sit in the same seat for each lecture. For most students, sitting in the same seat is probably a good idea, just for the advantage of getting to know a bunch of others who are probably going to sit in the same place too. However, you should sit wherever you feel most comfortable and where you think you will be able to stay focused during lectures.

Fourth, as with all classes, try your best not to arrive to class late or leave early. Quite frankly, this can be really rude. When you arrive late or leave early everyone notices—this puts the spotlight on you. In addition, when you come in late or leave early it interferes with the instructor's lecture. Instructors automatically look to see who is coming in late or leaving early and it throws instructors off their lecturing rhythm. If you ever get the chance to lecture in front of a class, you will find that getting off your rhythm is really a problem and can impact the flow of the lecture in a big way, especially when you lose your place just as you were about to make an important point. Of course, sometimes things are beyond your control, so if you must arrive late or leave early do it as quietly as possible, in a way where you will hardly be noticed. Don't come late and then walk all the way to the front of class. If you come in late, sit in a seat near where you entered the classroom. Two other quick points: 1) you might want to explain to your instructor about why you came to class late or left early; and 2) if you can, let your instructor know beforehand of your late arrival plans or that you must leave early. (Some large lecture classes have teaching assistants who consult a seating chart to take attendance. In these classes, you might want to let the TA know, also.)

STUDENT VOICES:

I think my biggest strategy was that if it was a relatively large class they had a TA ... I got to know that TA because really they're like a mediator between the students and the professor. That's who you're going to talk to if you have any discrepancies about homework or tests.

Fifth, never be afraid to ask a question or make a comment during class. Too often students think that this will annoy instructors of large classes—typically, this is not true. Despite the size of the class, almost all instructors like to entertain questions and comments during class. Go for it! Hearing questions from the class provides the instructor with a nice change-up from the lecture—it can be hard to lecture for an hour or more with no class participation. In addition, when students ask questions it allows the instructor to know both that students are engaged in the lecture and whether there is a need for additional examples or details about the content. In our experience, whatever you have to ask is something others in the class are wondering about also. Even though a large class will contain a lot of students, overcome your fear of speaking in a large class. What is the worst thing that will happen if you speak up in a large class? The instructor doesn't call on you? Possible. That the instructor might laugh at your question? Highly unlikely. Therefore, take the risk. We think you will find that the result will be very positive.

Sixth, talk to your instructor. As we said above you might get a chance to talk to your instructor if you sit near the front of the large classroom or arrive early. Even if you don't sit there, all instructors have office hours, and you should feel free to stop by to talk about class or other issues. With regard to the latter, for large classes in your major, you might want to discuss something interesting you heard about that is related to the class or your major, or talk about careers in your chosen field. You and your professor might even share a hobby or know the same person. Instructors will not know everyone in a large class, but the more contact you have with them, the better the chance that they will know you. Quick hint: Remind instructors of your name each time you interact because it may take them a while to learn your name with so many students in the classroom. As a practical matter, interacting with your instructor may help as you move forward with your career plans. You never know if you will need a letter of recommendation or if there is an opportunity to get involved with their research.

Finally, come to your large classes prepared and ready to learn and actively take notes. Also, you might decide that the large class format necessitates taking photos of various PowerPoint slides instructors present. Check with the instructor to make sure this is okay. A positive attitude will probably lead you to like your large classes more, to learn more, to do better in the class, and to find that class time zips by!

QUESTIONS

1. Is there anything about a large class that appeals to you? What?

2. What can you think of that will motivate you to sit close to the front of a large class?

3. Do you think it is wrong for colleges and universities to offer large classes? Why?

FIGURE CREDITS

SMALL CLASSES AND SEMINARS

Once classes start meeting on campus, you will discover that class sizes vary widely. Different sections of the same course will have different enrollments based on when they are scheduled. Saying this another way, classes range in size across a wide continuum from very large to tiny. As discussed in Chapter 11, the large lecture courses in community colleges and universities may have hundreds of students and are populated most often by first-year students taking general education requirements. Generally, class sizes decrease as you move from first and second year courses to your junior and senior years—when students are taking more courses in their major. In this chapter, we examine the smaller classes generally, and how the student and instructor roles may differ with some special variations of smaller classes.

Small courses could consist of 5, 15, 25 or just about any number of students between two and perhaps 50. From a definitional point of view, there is no standard of *small class* size, and faculty in different departments and colleges have different opinions about small class boundaries. In one department, 35 might be considered a large class, but in another department or college, between 75 and 100 students could be considered small. More important than the absolute number of students (e.g., whether you have 10 or 48 students in your class) are these two considerations:

- What are the differences in how faculty approach teaching small and large enrollment courses?

- How might your role as a student be different in small versus large enrollment courses?

HOW FACULTY APPROACH TEACHING SMALL AND LARGE CLASSES

In large enrollment courses, faculty primarily lecture. Because of theater-style seating in many large lecture halls, it is not usually possible for instructors to assign students to groups and have the groups work on some activity in class. (However, in some newly constructed classroom buildings, smaller rooms around a large screen for the instructor's presentation will allow for this.) Instructors of large classes, by necessity, teach in a somewhat different style than teachers with many fewer students.

Fig 12.1

Unlike large lecture courses that sweep across, or survey, a broad landscape of material but without great depth, small classes allow students and faculty to delve deeper into a particular topic, area, or problem. As a senior, your departmental major may require a *capstone* course where you will develop a special project or paper that helps consolidate and illuminate the learning that you have acquired during your college years. As you might expect, the faculty–student involvement is greater in this type of small course, where enrollment will be kept quite small intentionally. This course might also be known as a *senior seminar*. Seminars are small courses where there tend to be less lecture and more active student participation. (Note, though, that generalizations are difficult, and the amount of lecture in a small class depends on the topic, instructor, and class size, too.)

STUDENT VOICES:

Once you get into the small classes, you obviously have to participate. You form a relationship with the professor and you see how important and imperative participation is.

The unstated goal of seminars is to assist students in developing the ability to analyze, evaluate, and perhaps synthesize information. Educators call it developing *critical thinking*. They will not want you believing everything you read, but hope they are instead teaching you to become a thinker who looks at facts, finds patterns, and can make independent decisions despite the positions held by others. In some majors and programs, seminars are offered for students in the final year of their program.

In seminars, you might be surprised at how closely the faculty read your papers and the extent of their comments. They may make suggestions and ask you revise your paper and submit it again for them to read. Their feedback is not designed to make you feel stupid, but a process to help you improve your ability to analyze and polish your written communications.

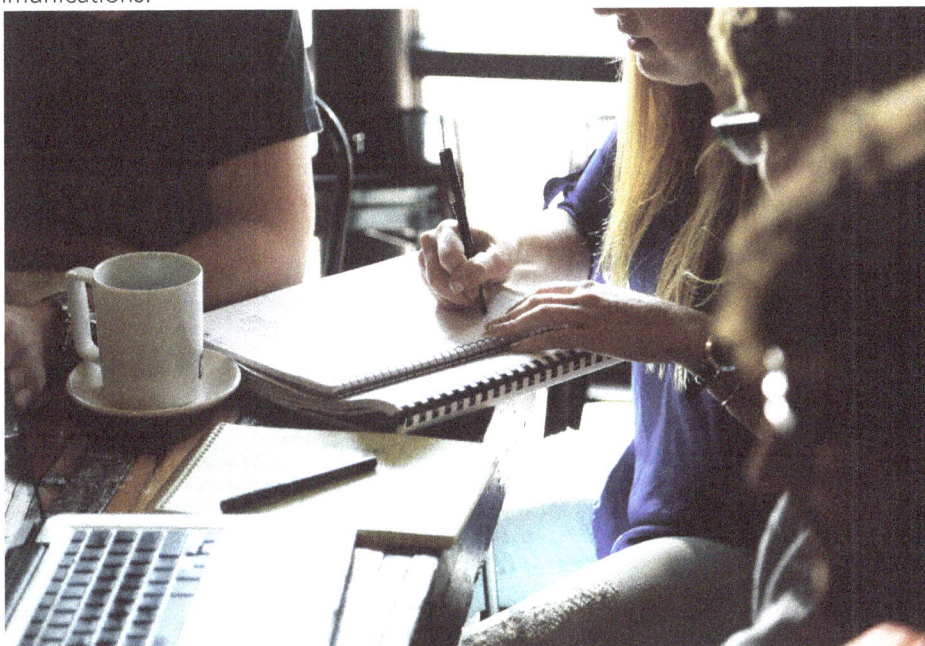

Fig 12.2

As a general rule, you will find that the smaller the class enrollment, the greater the likelihood that you will participate in certain in-class activities like discussions, brain-storming, debates, reflecting, writing papers, and engaging in small task or problem-solving groups.

Small groups teach students how to work together cooperatively—how to give and receive constructive criticism and feedback. You may be asked to review drafts of papers that your peers have written and to critique them and indicate areas that need attention. In small groups, you will have opportunities to teach other students and may even be motivated to expend more effort than you would ordinarily, so as not to be embarrassed by a student reading your paper or by letting your team members down.

Instructors of courses with small enrollments likely still lecture as a primary pedagogy but probably less than, or at least not as often as in the larger classes. In smaller classes, students spend proportionately more time discussing, debating, and thinking creatively about the readings and problems. Instructors act more like a guide or a facilitator. They will direct questions to you and might even play devil's advocate to see how you will think yourself out of a corner. The questions asked in class will not be about things you can memorize (like what famous battle was fought in 1815?). And the questions will not always have a single correct answer. In fact, what's often valued in these classes is your unique interpretation. For example, the instructor in a literature class might ask why, in your opinion, did an author bring another character into the plot at a particular point? Or, the instructor might ask, did the foreshadowing of the conflict that arose midway through the story telegraph the ending? In smaller classes, you really can't snooze.

HOW IS THE STUDENT'S ROLE DIFFERENT IN SMALL CLASSES?

If the student's role in large lecture classes is characterized as primarily passive learning (and that may not be entirely fair), then the student's role in small classes is much more likely to involve active learning. Imagine this situation: In your second meeting of a small class of 12 students, the instructor has everyone form their chairs into a circle and then starts asking around the circle: "What did you get out of the readings today?" Or, "What do you think the author should have done differently?"

What would you do if you hadn't read the assignment? Do you think the instructor would notice?

Small classes are intimate. The instructor knows your name, definitely knows when you're absent, makes a lot of eye contact with you, and knows when you are prepared to discuss assigned readings and when you aren't. You cannot hide behind other students or "forget" to bring your assignment to class without getting a skeptical look from the instructor. You will find that you must keep up with the readings and the assignments. That means you must do your reading before class, not after. You must participate if you hope to receive a reasonable grade.

Let's talk about participation. In small classes you are expected to participate regularly and often. This does not mean whenever you feel like it, whenever you have had time to prepare, or three or four times a semester. To *participate* could mean to make a contribution to the discussion at least once every class meeting (depending upon the number of students and the instructor) or it could mean you need to comment frequently each meeting. If the instructor does not clarify what kind of participation is expected when going over the syllabus, then you should ask about his or her expectations. A portion of your grade (possibly 10 or 15%) could be riding on your level of participation. However, prepare yourself for an answer that may not be quantitative. The answer you receive may not be as simple as three times a meeting but may rest on the quality of your comment. For instance, consider these three comments: 1) "Will we get to take a break today?"

2) "When will we get our break?" and 3) "How long do we have on the break?" If you were the instructor, would you consider those three questions as making a contribution to the class discussion?

If you are uncomfortable raising your hand and asking a question in front of a large group, you may find that you are much more comfortable talking in a small group—and you should have more opportunities to share your ideas. Some might argue that small classes prepare you for real life, when you will need to serve on committees and in various task groups. Whether that is true or not, at least in the small class you will very likely observe others, and see how to diplomatically disagree when you need to, or offer suggestions on how to improve a paper, project, or presentation. You may also experience someone not being a good role model for tactful communication and students not doing their part in a shared project. You will learn from both good and poor examples.

STUDENT VOICES:

A small seminar class is more about engaging and actively speaking ... having your own opinions and putting them forward and expressing yourself on more of an intimate level.

What does it take to succeed in small classes? Here are several suggestions:

- Always be prepared. Don't fall behind in your readings and assignments.

- Participate in discussions frequently

- Take a stab at answering questions even if you are unsure that your answer is right. Sometimes talking through what you know sharpens your thinking and allows you to see something that wasn't obvious earlier.

- If you love to participate, be careful not to dominate the discussions. Let others share their opinions, too.

- If you are afraid to talk in front of other students, realize that many students feel the same way. Turn your courage up and speak anyway! It will get easier the next time, and the time after that.

- Learn from the other students; get to know them.

If you are passionate about your major or special interest, you will very likely find that a seminar or small class on a topic you love is fun and an opportunity to acquire more depth in the subject. There is absolutely no reason to avoid small classes. To have a well-rounded education, you need a good mixture of both the smaller enrollment and the larger enrollment courses. Small classes are qualitatively different from the larger ones, but both types of courses have their strengths. Take small classes on topics you know nothing about but where you hear that the instructor is excellent. And apply yourself! Don't waste your education by learning only what comes across your cell phone.

QUESTIONS

1. Would you prefer lecture-type classes or smaller classes with in-class group activities? Why?

2. Would your answer to the first question change if the course involved your favorite subject? Why?

3. If you were an instructor, what type of course you would most like to teach? Why?

FIGURE CREDITS

Figure 12.1: escolaespai, "Small Class," https://pixabay.com/en/class-classroom-professor-student-377117/.
Figure 12.2: StartupStockPhotos, "Seminar," https://pixabay.com/en/startup-meeting-brainstorming-594090/.

ONLINE EDUCATION

Should you take an online course? To answer this question you need to keep in mind that when you go to college, there are many types of courses you can take. However, they have one thing in common: you, your classmates, and the instructor are all in the same room at the same time. Because of this, these traditional courses are typically referred to as "face-to-face" courses. However with the expanding internet, the past 20 years has seen tremendous growth in online education as an alternative way to teach college courses. Given that you do not have to be in a specific location on campus to take online courses (in fact, you might be some distance away), online courses are typically viewed as *distance education* or *distance learning*.

There are a few quick details and terms you should be aware of when thinking about taking online courses. First, online courses vary as to how much of the course is taught online. Some online courses present everything online: readings, quizzes, exams, interaction with peers, and the instructor—everything. There are, however, some online courses referred to as *hybrids*, which present some parts of the course online and present other parts face-to-face, in a classroom. Similarly, in some hybrid courses you can take your exams at home via your laptop and in others you need to travel to campus or a proctored site.

Second, online courses are typically discussed in terms of synchronicity. If an online course is totally *synchronous*, it means the entire class is working in unison, similar to a face-to-face class. These courses have lectures presented online at or about the same time every week, and quizzes and exams are taken and due on the same date for all students. Conversely, a course may be totally *asynchronous*, where all students participate on their own schedule. In asynchronous courses, each student moves through the content based on their own specific schedule. Some students may like to move fast, some slow, and there are some students who move between the two extremes. These asynchronous courses allow the student to work at 2:00 in the morning or 11:00 p.m., seven days a week. As you can imagine, you also see courses that combine aspects of both a synchronous and an asynchronous course. For example, a course may allow students to go through the content for each unit at their own pace, but all students take the exam for that unit at a set time. Thus, in this type of hybrid, you never have students that are too far ahead or too far behind the others.

Fig 13.1

Now that you understand the basic types of online courses, you may realize their vast potential. Consider the issue of scheduling flexibility. If you have a full-time job or family responsibilities (e.g., children, elderly parent) that keep you from attending traditional classes on a campus, online classes allow you to take one or more classes that meet your busy schedule. For example, you might not be able to take a traditional course that meets in on campus from 11:00–11:50 a.m. on Monday, Wednesday, and Friday. However, an online course can be accessed after you get home from your job, or when your children have gone to sleep, or when you finished feeding your farm animals (for those who live in rural areas). What adds to the flexibility is that online classes allow you to be in a totally different location than the college offering the course. You might live in Kentucky, but the online class you want to take is offered by a college in Hawaii. Regardless of where you are and where the online course originates, the internet allows you to take the class and to communicate 24/7 with your classmates and the instructor.

Another big advantage of online courses is that they can (depending on the school) cost less than face-to-face courses. You need to keep in mind that courses taught on a campus cost a lot. Besides paying a full-time faculty member's salary, there are a lot of extra costs (typically taken for granted) associated with a face-to-face classes. These include things like maintenance costs for classrooms and for the campus as a whole, heating and cooling the campus, electricity for everything from parking garages to bathrooms, support of the library, and on and on. In addition, when you take an online course you save money because you are not paying for things like commuting to campus (whether by car or public transportation), parking, tolls (if you live in certain locations with toll or bridge tolls), and dorm fees. Also, your car-repair costs should be less.

Finally, in the pro column for online courses is that they offer you a different kind of flexibility—flexibility in how you obtain a degree. Online courses can help you to complete a degree in conjunction with face-to-face courses, and there are a number of degrees that can be completed with just online courses.

This all sounds great, but as you can imagine there are also arguments against taking online courses. First, some have argued that online courses get away from the very essence of being in college, namely interacting in a spontaneous way with classmates and instructors in a classroom on a college campus. You will miss out on the live learning that occurs as you and your fellow students talk before and after class, as you walk to class, or sit in the coffee shop discussing things like the current course or other courses that might interest you. It would be hard to argue that online courses lead to more contact with faculty or students. They simply don't.

Second, online courses are not for everyone. They require being extremely organized and motivated to keep up with the demands of the course. There is no one looking you in the eye and telling you that need to go to class or reminding you to turn in assignments. It really is all on you. Some individuals can motivate themselves to accomplish all of the online course work and are great at organizing their time, but others find online course to be overwhelming. For those in the latter category, it may simply be that taking an online class is too different from the classroom structure that students have experienced in the past. Supporting the idea that online courses are not a good fit for every student, data show that online classes have a relatively high rate of students not complete the classes.

FACULTY VOICES:

Schedule time into your calendar to do your work daily and stick to it! Time management is one of the hardest things about distance learning.

Fig 13.2

Third, if an online class isn't being offered by your school, you need to be aware that some online courses are not legitimate, and may be claiming to offer much more than they deliver. This will not be true for an online course offered by established colleges or universities. However, a number of for-profit schools and programs whose status is unclear offer online courses. Keep in mind that before signing up for an online course, you should determine that the school and program are accredited. That means the college has been officially recognized as meeting certain official requirements (e.g., regarding material that is taught, teaching faculty). The importance of being accredited is so that if you take an online course other colleges and employers will likely recognize it as a valid course. Be wary of schools and programs that do not offer some type of student support. Despite offering the course online, the school or program should be able to offer assistance with things like technology and library resources. With regard to the latter, do they even have a library? Not having a physical campus, an actual brick and mortar library and full-time faculty should be a red flag. Finally, to avoid online scams from diploma mills (i.e., phony schools that sell diplomas), don't allow the school or program to pressure you to sign up, guarantee you a degree, or tell you a degree can be earned in just a few weeks or months. Be especially cautious if you are asked for a lot of tuition up front or you are asked to take out loans to cover tuition costs. As you have heard before with other businesses, if it sounds too good to be true, it probably is not true.

A fourth caution against online courses is that the course may have hidden technology expenses. Of course, to take an online course you need a computer and good internet access to connect to the course. This may require upgrading your computer (or even buying a new computer) and your internet access may need upgrading. You could get access to a course via a computer at a local public library, but this may lead to problems for you, given the limited hours of libraries and the competition to use public computers. With all of this in mind, be sure you know what technology you need before signing up for an online course, not after the course gets started. Don't be afraid to ask questions before you sign up.

FACULTY VOICES:

Make sure you have a source for a backup computer and internet in case yours goes out. If you are trying to meet a deadline, you need to have a plan already in place if something goes wrong. A local library is usually a good option as a backup.

Fifth, in general online courses offer a great deal of scheduling flexibility. However, it is again important to make sure you know exactly how the course operates before taking it. For example, the online course may be a hybrid course that requires being on campus a certain day and time every other week. Or, the exams for an online course may be given at a special proctoring center far from your home. If you can deal with these structural aspects of the course, all is good; however, your personal schedule may keep you from taking anything other than an online course that is 100% online.

Finally, not all majors may be available or sufficiently covered by online courses or online degrees. For example, some majors related to health care are better taken in a face-to-face class environment. Other courses require working with certain materials (e.g., plants, animal specimens) or equipment (e.g., microscopes) that are more accessible in a traditional classroom. If you are strongly considering an online program from a for-profit organization, check it out with someone who is already working in the field you're interested in. Ask, for instance, if a degree from the program you're considering would make it possible for their company or organization to hire you. Be a good consumer, and as discussed above, check things out before you commit to anything.

In the end, deciding whether to take an online course can be difficult. However, if you take your time and consider all of the issues, as well as talk to others (e.g., your college academic advisors), you should be in a position to make a well-informed choice. And one last suggestion: in online and hybrid courses it is more difficult for instructors to get to know you. Nonetheless, just because you don't meet the instructor in person doesn't mean you should feel that the effort you expend should be any less than in a face-to-face class.

> **STUDENT VOICES:**
>
> *I found that the quality of a distance learning class really depends on how present the professor makes you feel. Because it's online, a lot of time they give you more resources or some of them email you directly and keep in touch with you that way.*

QUESTIONS

1. What are the chances you will take an online class?

2. Should students be allowed to get their college degree by only taking online courses? Why?

3. What would you do to stay on track if you took an online course?

FIGURE CREDITS

THE ART OF LISTENING & TAKING NOTES

What skills would you list as essential to your success as a college student? Most likely your list includes being able to communicate effectively, both orally and in writing. Your list probably includes quantitative skills, recognizing that math and statistical reasoning have become fundamental to many majors and careers. How to make the most of library resources, which is now termed information literacy, would make your list, as would computer skills, time management, and basic study skills. Interestingly, a skill unlikely to be on your list is one that seems so basic you may take for granted that you have already mastered it: listening!

It is quite easy to underemphasize the importance of listening skills, but to prosper in college it is in your best interest to think carefully about how to listen better. Unlike high school, much more of your time in class will demand good listening skills. The messages that you need to listen to, especially in large lecture situations, are much more complicated than what you experienced in high school. Both the amount of information and the pace at which teachers deliver that information in lectures is well beyond what occurs in high school.

Simply stated, your instructors would prefer that you not miss a single word. You will be required to exhibit a disciplined, intentional approach to listening that reflects a different attitude to its purpose. You will need to do whatever you can to help prepare yourself to be a good listener. To that end, let us explore a few basic strategies you can employ to be certain that your ability to listen is at the highest level. Start with the simple principle: hearing is not the same as listening.

An obvious point is that in order to listen to a lecture effectively you must be in class to hear the lecture! Most college and university classes meet only two or three times each week, which means that you must comprehend and learn more dense content during lecture classes than you experienced in high school. A 50-minute university lecture contains much more information than you typically experienced in 50-minute high school classes. The pace at which that information is being delivered in a college lecture does not compare to what occurs in high school. To miss one lecture in college could be the

Fig 14.1

equivalent of missing an entire week in high school. And do not think that reading your friends' notes for lectures you miss is equivalent to being in the lecture and doing your own listening.

A good place to begin being a better listener is developing good habits for what you do and do not do before coming to class. It seems a cliché, but basic healthy living is essential to academic success. Practicing a regular, healthy routine is one of the best ways you can transition into college. Getting enough sleep and developing regular sleep habits are critical; sleeping for the same number of hours each night and going to sleep and waking at the same time each day offers an invaluable foundation for academic work. To be a good student requires energy. You cannot listen effectively to a lecture if you are falling asleep or so tired that you cannot concentrate on what you are hearing. Listening is a cognitive skill that requires your mind to actively encode and decode complex verbal messages. Hearing words is not the same as understanding ideas. Likewise, healthy eating is essential. Mind and body are one, but students often get off track by failing to adhere to healthy diets and healthy eating habits: fried chicken wings and melted cheese at 2:00 a.m. is probably not something that highly successful students indulge in that often!

Another aspect to good preparation for listening is staying up to date with the content of the course by doing all readings and assignments as specified. Any reading you can do in advance of a lecture is especially beneficial. Consult the course syllabus and anticipate the material being covered in the next lecture, and if possible, examine any readings or other resources you can access pertinent to the content of the pending lecture before attending.

Then there is the actual act of listening. An obvious recommendation is to avoid all distractions. Daydreaming, thinking about what you will do that night, what you will eat for lunch, or how you can meet that intriguing student sitting next to you may be normal human behavior, but these kinds of thoughts are distractions. To listen well, you have to focus all of your attention on what the instructor is saying, block out distractions, and think about what you are hearing. Again, processing a lecture is not simply about recognizing words; it requires you to comprehend the ideas being communicated, which demands that you think about what is being said.

The same principle holds for other forms of distraction. Do not text or email, surf the web, or do other work while listening to a lecture. There is a grand fallacy circulating today that it is possible to become good at multitasking. Many students argue that they can listen to a lecture while also texting their parents. More generally, there are those among us who believe we can drive our cars as well when texting or talking on the phone as when we are not doing so.

There is now overwhelming evidence that multitasking is not possible: We cannot do two or more things at the same time as well as we can do each separately. Psychological research has established that when we think we are multitasking well, for instance texting and listening to a lecture at the same time, we are actually shifting attention continuously between the two tasks; one moment we concentrate on texting and the next we attempt to listen to the lecture. So, anytime you spend texting during a lecture you are failing to listen, and you will miss content. A good habit to form is turning off your smartphone and any computer device that you do not need during a lecture.

One tricky problem is that in some classes, instructors allow or even encourage taking notes with a laptop or tablet. If you do that, limit yourself to taking notes; do not email, check social media, or browse the internet shopping for shorts. It is very difficult for students to resist these distractions, which is why many teachers are now prohibiting use of electronic devices during class. In addition, there is evidence that notes written in longhand produce better memory than typewritten notes. Of course, there will be some classes for which these devices enhance learning, but then you need to rely on your own discipline. Once again we confront an essential proposition: You will determine your success in college!

Listening and note taking go together. It is not sufficient, in most cases, to listen without recording what you comprehend. Some written record is necessary, one that can be viewed later as part of your overall study strategy. The goal, of course, is to incorporate the ideas presented in a lecture into your private archive of knowledge. Simply put, you need to both understand the ideas presented and store that understanding in memory. Think of your notes as a tool that helps you achieve that task. You will use your notes to help organize and establish your memories, and you will also use them to test yourself with respect to what you have and have not memorized. Accordingly, accurate, useful notes are imperative in lecture-based courses.

As with other academic skills, students rely on some proven strategies to get the greatest benefits from note taking. First, determine whether your teacher makes his lecture outlines

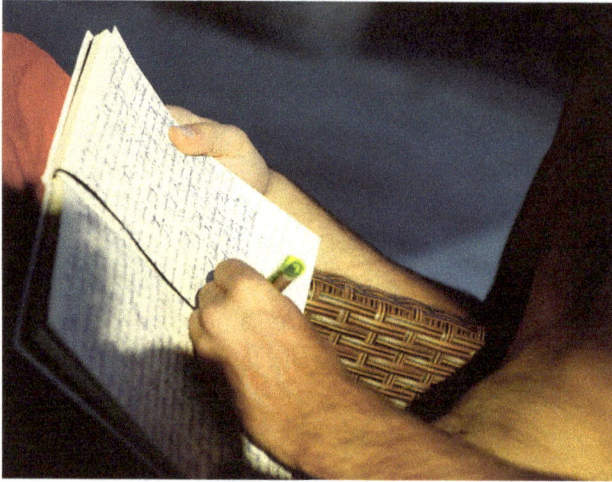

Fig 14.2

and other materials (e.g., pictures, explicit definitions, charts, graphs) available before or perhaps after a lecture. The common use of electronic presentations during lectures enables teachers to present vivid visual information during the lecture, and those materials can also be made available to students for viewing outside of class. Instructors differ in terms of their policies regarding access to these materials, so it is incumbent on you to know that policy. Equally important is the teacher's policy regarding audio recording of lectures. Some instructors allow you to tape record their lecture, but others do not. Know their policy and adhere to it!

Regardless of whether you have access to lecture materials, your likely notes need to include information beyond visual aids. What teachers say and what they present visually are usually somewhat different. No quality teacher will simply present words on a screen that they read to the class. A lecture usually uses visual materials to outline the lecture or present specific detailed information, such as a psychology professor showing and explaining a diagram of the functional anatomy of the brain, or a history professor explaining a map showing battles of the Civil War.

There are a few well-established techniques that you can use to enhance the quality of your note taking and do not detract from effective listening. One simple idea is to use a loose-leaf binder that enables you to remove individual pages. In terms of explicit note taking, do not attempt to right down everything your teacher says. Rather, listen to and comprehend the main ideas and points. Then, write something brief that represents those ideas using abbreviations, brief phrases, and individual words that you can later decode and expand. Do not attempt to record complete sentences, nor is it recommended to use a highlighter pen while taking notes. Generally, you want your notes to express what you understand from the lecture in your own words, not the words of the teacher.

FACULTY VOICES:

I like students to be concentrating on making higher-level connections in class and less focused on making a transcript of what I say.

STUDENT VOICES:

As a freshman you think you should only be copying down the PowerPoint notes, but it's more important to listen to what is actually being said by the professor because they add on a lot of stuff that is not even written on the PowerPoint slides.

Other simple strategies include starting each lecture on a new page that includes the date of the lecture, leaving spaces to add additional information at a later time, and being as neat as possible while writing quickly. You may want to explore explicit note taking strategies, such as the Cornell Method. Books and articles describing these strategies in detail are easy to find. In some cases, it is what you do not do that matters most. For example, a common tragedy shared by too many students is that they are unable to read their own notes. So do not write such that you cannot read what you have written. For that and other reasons, let us turn to another aspect of taking notes: processing the notes after a lecture as part of your study strategy.

It is usually not enough to take notes and then reread those notes as your study technique. The more valuable approach is to reprocess the ideas represented in your notes. There are a number of effective techniques you can use to improve the quality of your raw notes. One strategy is to recopy your notes, but the goal should not be simply to have a neater version of your original notes. It is better to use recopying as a way of expanding and organizing the ideas in your notes.

To that end, put your notes into a formal outline format (e.g., I. A. 1. a., b. c, II. A.), draw or redraw figures and charts, use different colored inks for different sections, and use highlighter pens to emphasize specific words as part of recopying lecture notes. These techniques not only create a better record of a lecture's ideas, but also engage your mind in processing those ideas. Transforming abbreviated notes into a more elaborate and better organized format requires you to process the ideas at a deeper level, which is actually what memory storage is about. By deeper processing, we mean for example, that you think about the idea related to a word or concept and not merely repeat the word to yourself over and over. Of course, *when* you recopy is critical. Usually it is necessary to recopy the same day or the day after your lecture to gain the most benefit. If you wait too long, you loose your memory of information you may not have included in your notes.

Another proven strategy is mind mapping. The goal here is to translate written notes into graphic diagrams that serve as conceptual maps for the ideas contained in a lecture. A good mind map presents ideas in relational terms (i.e., which ideas are connected and which are more important?) using shapes, key words, color, and connecting lines between ideas that are conceptually related. The diagram below illustrates a mind map for outlining the basic functions of the human mind. Accordingly, the creation of a mind map requires considerable effort; you must "think" a mind map not just draw one.

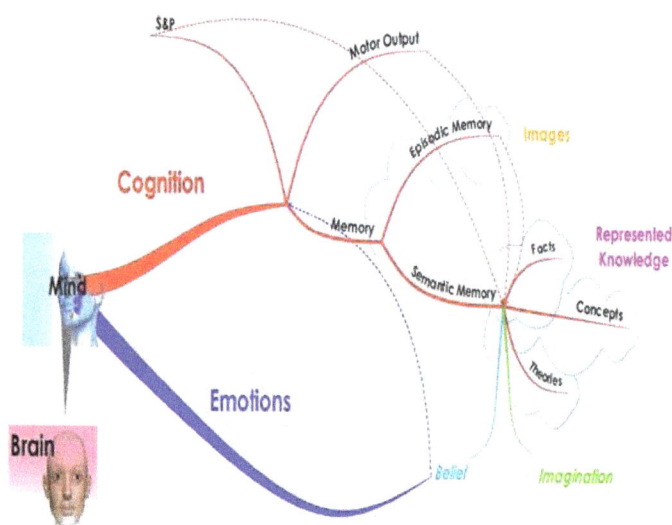

Fig 14.3

Figure 14.3: Created using i-MindMap 5.

QUESTIONS

1. Think about the courses in high school that required you to take notes. What worked for you in these classes with respect to note taking?

2. How do you intend to manage distractions during lectures?

3. Try creating a mind map of your family.

FIGURE CREDITS

Figure 14.1: evanst10000, "Classroom," https://pixabay.com/en/teaching-learning-classroom-661748/.
Figure 14.2: tiburi, "Taking Notes," https://pixabay.com/en/note-writing-pen-paper-hand-write-1547506/.
Figure 14.3: Created using i-MindMap 5.

DEALING WITH READING ASSIGNMENTS

Will there be more reading in college than in high school? You bet! Chapters in textbooks will be 25 to 30 pages on average with some running to 40 or 50 and the professor may assign two or more chapters before the next class meeting. That's one class. In another, you may be expected to read a novel within a week. In the third class, you may have to wade through multiple websites to find the best case study to present for a class project, and you still have two other courses to go. Yes, there will be reading, and plenty of it.

How will you manage all of it? Students often assume that if they don't do the reading, the instructor won't know. Wrong. Instructors who pose questions about the readings in class can always tell when students drop their heads, divert their eyes or when they get an excited look that communicates "I know, I know!" It is true that in a large class, you may not be called on and no one might be the wiser if you haven't done the reading on any particular

Fig 15.1

day. However, the material still must be digested. Every day, every week it goes unread, the further you are getting behind. Is it easier to read 150 pages at a time before the exam on Wednesday or to keep current by reading 30 pages a night? In college, you get to decide for yourself.

Your instructor can also identify the readers from the nonreaders through graded assignments. These can include your instructor 1) conducting a pop quiz or posing several questions electronically for you to answer in a large lecture class, or 2) including questions on exams that come directly from your readings. Some students are gamblers, believing they can sense when a quiz might arrive and plan to read just before that happens. Other students stay current with the reading. What will be your strategy?

Our recommendation, of course, would be that you take your readings assignments seriously. If this is the type of student you want to be, then here are some suggestions for how to get the most out of your reading.

Preview: When you are ready to read, open the book or your computer and skim through the chapter. Read the title, any overview or abstract, and each heading in the chapter. Look at each table, chart, and diagram. Think of this effort as watching a movie trailer: you want to see what the chapter or reading is about. What mystery is it trying to tell you about? What information does it hold? This preview will let you know whether the reading is over familiar territory—whether you can read it at a high rate of speed, or whether it is dense and obscure, requiring a much slower pace.

Involve Yourself in the Reading: Reading without involvement is wasting about 70% of your effort. Why? Because you won't retain much of what you read. In order to preserve what you read in your memory circuits, you must participate in the reading; you must do more than just letting your eyes dance across the page. For instance, if there are vocabulary words that you don't know, use the glossary at the end of the chapter or back of the book (or a dictionary). Or, Google the terms to look them up. Take notes about what you are learning. Are there steps or principles that the author lists? If they seem important, write them in a notebook and use a highlighter so that you can find them easily when you come back to read this material again. (Note: in highlighting, it is important to highlight just the important passages. When you are finished with your yellow highlighting, most of the page *should not* be yellow.)

If you don't want to write down notes as you read, then at least write down the concepts or key words that you might want to come back to later; you could also make note of a concept (e.g., molecular weight) and jot down a page number beside it for quick reference later.

Another way to get involved in the material is to pose questions to yourself as you read. Ask yourself, "Is this portion of the reading of major importance, or minor importance?" Items of major importance might involve foundational knowledge, which could likely be on future quizzes and exams. For example, if you are learning about *imprinting* (i.e., when newborn members of one species attach or bond with another during a critical period of development), it is important to understand what the term means. Knowing that the originator of the term, Konrad Lorenz, was born in 1903 is of much less (minor) importance for understanding the concept. You can also ask the question, "Is it likely I will see this on a quiz or exam?" If you believe you will, take the time to make a flashcard or highlight it, or even note TQ (for "test question") in the margin of your book or photocopied reading.

Authors of textbooks recognize that students may not know how to distinguish important material from the sentences and paragraphs that provide context, or add some refinement or nuance to the reading. To assist you, authors typically use **bold fonts** for key words, terms, and concepts that they want you to pay special attention to. Don't skip over and ignore these. Make a point to record somewhere every term that is in bold font. Also, textbook authors often define key terms and provide summaries of important concepts at the end of each chapter.

Another clue that material might be important to remember is when authors give illustrations or examples of concepts. To actively engage with the material, think about the examples and see if you can create another one yourself. If you are not sure your example works or fits, then ask your instructor or TA at the next class meeting. The instructor will be impressed! Don't be afraid to ask such questions. Instructors want you to be *exactly that involved* with the material! It shows you are eager to learn.

FACULTY VOICES:

When you come across a word you don't know for sure, look it up and note how it was used. Incorporate it into your own vocabulary. Devour the next reading. Relish it. Be proud of each thing well read. You will soon see the difference in how you think and what you see and understand around you.

Review: Thinking about the material you read is critical for encoding it in memory. Reading 15 pages from your text and then watching two hours of *My Cat From Hell* will not help you retain what you have read. Instead, after you have read, look over your notes of what you thought was important. As you consider these ideas, did you leave anything out? If your notes are too succinct or too wordy, will the main point that you want to remember be clear later on? You might also want to examine the key words and terms you have listed and quiz yourself to see if you can explain them or recall the examples associated with them. If you took no notes, quickly skim what you have read. Is there anything you should note or highlight?

Some experts advise against reading 30 to 50 pages in one sitting, but rather, suggest "chunking" it by dividing the reading into 10 or 15 page chunks. At the end of each chunk, you should look over your notes and self-test, or simply stand up and stretch or walk around the room. But as you stretch or walk, think about what you just read. Why is the reading or the passages important? How does it fit into a larger picture? How will you remember it? If questions come to mind as you do this self-review, then write them down for later when you share them with a study group, or ask them of the instructor.

All of this good advice is abbreviated in an approach used in many schools across the country. Known as the SQ4R method, it has been tweaked and modified over the years, but its core—involving students in what they are reading—has remained constant. A brief explanation is provided next. Try it. See if

Fig 15.2

your reading comprehension improves.

The SQ4R Method

- *S*urvey the material. Scan, skim, or skip through the chapter to determine what it is all about. What do the headings, subheadings, and graphics tell you about it?

- *Q*uestion. What questions do you have? Write them down. Turn major headings into questions. For instance, "Major Threats to the Internal Validity of a Study" becomes "What are the major threats to the internal validity of studies?" Asking questions like this help you see if you remember what you just read. Ask who, what, when, where, and why.

- *R*$_1$ead. Read for understanding. Look for the answers to your questions. Make notes about the examples or concepts that you don't understand.

- *R*$_2$ecite. Read the sections that you don't understand aloud. Read the section again if you don't know the answers to your questions or if something is unclear.

- R_3eview. After your first full reading of the material, review it again later. Write down the vocabulary items, concepts, and so forth that you need to work on. Make flash cards for yourself. Create a quiz over the material; have a friend create one for you.

- R_4elate. Think of examples related to what you are learning. Reflect on the reading. Go beyond the text. Check with the TA or instructor to see if that is a good application. Imagine ways that you will remember the content that is difficult to recall. Make an acronym or mnemonic device for remembering.

If the SQ4R approach seems too involved for you, try simplifying it by following the simple mnemonic, *3Rs*.

- **R**ead the material thoroughly, trying to understand the point of each paragraph, what the author is trying to explain.

- **R**ecord notes, questions, and keywords/terms/concepts that you think are important. Write them down, make lists.

- **R**ecall and reflect upon what you have read and noted. Even better, try to recite aloud what you have learned in reading that chunk of pages.

MISTAKES STUDENTS MAKE REGARDING READING

College students often have very busy lives. We instructors know that. However, just because you are involved in a sorority or fraternity, have a part-time job, and are starting a new relationship does not give you an excuse to skip reading and be unprepared for class. So here's some very practical advice about reading assignments:

- Don't get behind. Stay current with your readings.

- If you have an enormous reading assignment and have very little time, then don't try to read every word in a 50-page chapter. Instead, focus on the bold and italicized fonts. Pay special attention to the headings and the first and last paragraphs of each section. If there are questions at the end of the text's chapter, review them to see if you have a good understanding of the material.

- Don't blow off the readings altogether and think that the instructor's PowerPoint slides will tell you everything you need to know. They won't.

- Don't go into an exam having read the material associated only with the terms listed on the study guide given you.

- Don't underestimate the importance of taking notes as you read. It is the repetition of writing these key concepts down that helps encode them into your memory. Yes, it is faster to read without taking notes, but it is easier to remember the material if you make notes about it.

- Do try to read in a place that is relatively quiet and free of distractions.

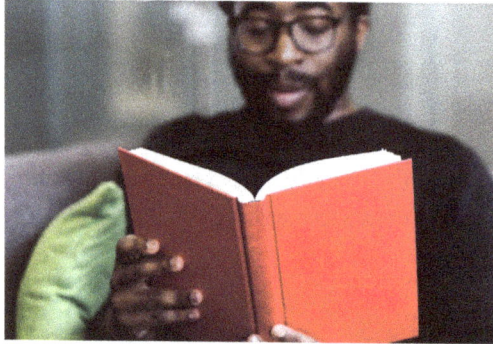

Fig 15.3

QUESTIONS

1. Do you read at different speeds for different types of material or do you read everything at the same speed? Do you think everything should be read at the same speed?

2. Do you feel that your reading speed is fast enough? If not, what can you do to improve it?

3. How important is having a strong vocabulary when reading? If you worry that your vocabulary isn't adequate, what can you do to strengthen it?

WRITING

Two skills essential to being a successful college student are writing and reading. It is difficult to imagine being able to function without some rudimentary foundation in each skill. Although both skills are critical, you may further develop these skills to different extents in college. Your reading can improve, but your writing *will* improve, and the undergraduate experience is structured to improve writing significantly. Unlike for reading, you are likely to take a writing course or a course that combines writing and oral communication during your first semester.

FACULTY VOICES:

There is no more important skill that being able to write well.
Throw yourself into the task.

The reason that most colleges and universities have explicit writing course requirements is that this skill is critical to both academic success and the jobs and careers for which a college education prepares you. From science and engineering, to business, health care, and the arts, good communication skills are in high demand, and writing is especially valuable to the modern workforce. Being able to write clearly and competently might determine who gets the job and who keeps it. Ironically, although with the advent of email, texting, and Twitter, people are writing more than ever before, the quality of writing has not necessarily improved with heavy use of these communication technologies. In fact, some claim that writing has deteriorated with the computer revolution: Doing something often does not mean that it is done well.

Beyond required courses in writing, many of your other classes will have writing assignments designed to help you learn the content of the course while also improving your skill as a writer. In many classes your course grade will be based in part on writing assignments. In addition, many teachers will use brief writing assignments at the beginning or end of a class as a strategy to help you think and learn. So, be prepared to write, and be prepared to learn to improve your writing.

Beyond elementary writing principles, as you move into your major you will develop domain-specific writing skills. For example, psychology majors learn to write in a style that adheres to professional standards of publications in psychology. Likewise, there is a specific kind of writing style that is used by business majors, another for engineers, and yet other styles for majors in the humanities. Each discipline has its own expectations for the kind of writing, the style of writing, and the formal standards of writing expected of students. These expectations apply to the writing you will do in courses within the major, but these standards also apply to the work you will do in careers and jobs associated with that major.

Fig 16.1

At this point, it is appropriate to mention one of the most important considerations of the writing process: *plagiarism*. In general, the academic enterprise rests on a foundation of core values. The most important of these values is academic honesty. Cheating on a test is one way to violate the academic honesty principle, and plagiarism is another. Much of what occurs in higher education involves sharing of ideas, from the scholarship practiced by your professors to the research and creative work that you do as a student, including the papers you write. It is essential that we give and receive credit for the ideas we share based on where those ideas originate. By definition, plagiarism occurs whenever an individual "steals" ideas from another individual or individuals. No one, student or professor, should present the ideas of another as if they were their own.

Although plagiarism in college usually arises in writing, realize that it can occur with any medium used to communicate ideas. Instances of plagiarism include stealing or passing off of another's ideas or words as one's own; failing to give credit to a source of ideas that you include in your own writing; and committing literary theft by presenting an idea or product that you obtained from an existing source as new and original. Many examples of plagiarism are obvious and self evident, but modern communication technologies have created some complicated challenges to understanding the boundaries of academic dishonesty. Accordingly, most first-year writing courses will spend time on this issue.

Given the emphasis placed on writing in higher education, it is in your best interest to adopt the right attitude, beyond your commitment to academic honesty. To that end, we suggest that as you transition to college you embrace the idea that you should do whatever you can to improve your writing throughout your undergraduate years. The benefits of that attitude will extend well beyond the college experience. It is therefore advisable to take advantage of all of the resources available to you. For example, most institutions offer some form of a writing center that provides explicit assistance to undergraduates. There may also be tutoring available at your institution that targets helping you with explicit writing assignments in individual courses. Find where these services are located, and use them!

It is also important to realize, however, that there is much that you can do on your own to become a better writer. Self improvement begins with how you actually approach writing. If you wait until the last minute to complete writing assignments, write them quickly merely to finish, and do not reread and edit your writing, you are not helping yourself. Good writing rarely comes to the page without effort and without the need to edit and revise. Most good writers accept that they need to produce multiple drafts; writing and revising repetitively until the best product emerges is the essence of good writing. A good rule of thumb is to never submit a paper that has not been revised at least twice, but you would be wise to plan on having even more drafts to ensure that your best work emerges.

FACULTY VOICES:

Improve your writing. You will end up thinking better, communicating better, and finding yourself more valued and depended upon.

Where you write also matters. If you sit in front of a TV or at table with a group of friends and attempt to write, you will probably discover that it is much more difficult to do the writing and your end product will be less than it could and should be. Writing requires deep concentration. You must avoid distractions and concentrate completely on the task of writing. You cannot multitask. On a related point, it will benefit you to develop good writing habits as early as possible. These habits should include defining a regular place at which you write (seek a quiet refuge), how much time you commit to a writing episode (the quality of your writing can deteriorate if you write for too long without a break), and the actual writing process you use. When writing extends over multiple sessions, some writers always begin a writing episode at the beginning of their document to ensure that they edit and revise thoroughly, but others start where they left off. Adopt a strategy that works for you, and commit to it. There is considerable value in using outlines and mind maps to organize your ideas before weaving words into sentences. A mind map is a graphical representation of ideas that displays conceptual relationships between ideas and the relative importance of each idea. A mind map uses geometric shapes, words, and pictures to succinctly represent complex groups of ideas.

There are also some simpler ways to help yourself become a better writer. For example, take advantage of the tools available to you. A dictionary and thesaurus are essential for all students. A writer's guide is also a good resource and you would benefit by buying one before you begin your college experience. It will serve as a constant guide and reference that you can consult often as you write. Many guides offer useful tips on good writing, as well as condensed summaries of rules of grammar. Spend sometime perusing a writer's guide to become more familiar with the mechanics of good writing. Many of these writing resources are now available electronically as 'apps' for smartphones and tablets.

Never assume that you have mastered writing, and never accept that what you write is perfect. Adhere to the constant improvement model; always seek to do better. One strategy you can use for that purpose is to share your writing and solicit feedback from others. We all have a blindness that precludes us from objectively evaluating our own writing. Be open to the criticism and advice of others. In the end, however, you must develop your own voice; your writing has to be yours.

In addition to explicit writing tools, related resources and strategies can improve your writing. One important consideration is your vocabulary. Again, do not assume that you know enough words. There are both print versions and electronic versions of resources to improve your vocabulary. One way to assert your commitment to being a successful student is to commit to increasing your vocabulary on a regular basis. It is not uncommon for excellent students to set a goal for themselves to add five or ten new words to their working vocabulary each week. Words are the core element for any writer, and having a more expansive vocabulary to rely on pays dividends that not only make you a better writer, but also make you a better thinker. Of course, the one danger to avoid here is being pretentious. Do not use a big word merely for the sake of using a big word. Do not be a sesquipedalian!

Fig 16.2

Finally, there is a simple way for you to become a better writer: Look for good writing by others. By reading regularly, beyond your core required reading, you will be able to recognize good writing and distinguish it from bad writing. Good writers are usually avid readers, and reading provides role models for writing excellence. Find a role model!

QUESTIONS

1. What is the longest and best thing you have written? Why do you think it is good?

2. Based on what you have read, who do you think is a good writer? What makes their writing good?

FIGURE CREDITS

Figure 16.1: StartupStockPhotos, "Writing with Yellow Pen," https://pixabay.com/en/write-plan-business-startup-593333/.
Figure 16.2: terimakasih0, "Writing in Book," https://pixabay.com/en/hands-writing-words-letter-working-1373363/.

WHAT IS STUDYING?

Let's start by identifying what does not constitute studying. When my son (Royse) was in high school and struggling with Algebra II, I stopped in his room the night before a big test. Much to my surprise, he had the television on, music playing, and his computer open. He was holding his pet white rat in one hand and his textbook in his lap, and approximately every 20 seconds or so, would flip a page. Periodically, he would say (and probably for my benefit), "We went over that." Flip. "Covered that." Flip. "Know that." Unbeknownst to Josiah, he was violating practically every important principle associated with studying effectively. Do you know why? More about this later.

Our term *study* has its origin in the Latin word stadium that translates as, eagerness, devotion, and zeal. So, ideally, a student would be eager to learn, devoted to acquiring more knowledge, and show zeal in applying the effort it took to become more learned. Synonyms for studying include scrutinizing, inspecting, examining, and considering. Do you see that these synonyms suggest the student must have his or her mind *engaged* in the material so that it can be thought about carefully, chewed on, weighed, and contemplated? In short, to study means interacting with the material. Does looking at a page, then turning it quickly to the next page, constitute studying?

In thinking about studying it is important to be aware that one of the greatest obstacles to succeeding in college is the fallacy that what you did in high school is all that you have to do in college in order to be a good student. Certainly, some of the ways you managed your academic success in high school will translate into success in college, but too many students are unprepared for the harsh lesson that college is not grade 13. Some of what worked in the past for you needs to be tweaked and significantly modified, but there are also new techniques that you will adopt in order to meet the new challenges that you will face.

Also, you need to understand that the learning that you will pursue in college is of two types: skills and knowledge. For each you will need to rely on teachers for assistance, but for each you will also need to perform actions in order to learn. For skills, practice is necessary. Once you acquire a basic understanding of how to do something (e.g., write a scientific paper, use a math formula, balance a chemical equation, create a computer program, construct an oral presentation using digital media), you need to practice the actions that define that skill. Academic skills, as with athletic skills, require time and effort. The basic elements of learning any skill are the same: repeat the actions that constitute the skill, obtain feedback on your performance, evaluate your performance in terms of where you are and where you want to be, and attempt to narrow the gap between the two. For skill learning, your teachers function more like coaches: they provide useful feedback and guidance on how to improve.

The greater challenge new undergraduates face involves knowledge-based learning. The basic purpose of the curriculum is to define the knowledge that is necessary to become a well-educated citizen and attain some level of expertise. As you learn, you build your personal reserve of knowledge in memory; think of this as creating your own knowledge archive. When you study, you add knowledge to your archive. For that to occur, you must understand the ideas covered in your classes. You cannot memorize ideas you do not understand, and it does you little good to understand an idea that you do not memorize.

A big question you may have about your memory is, "What exactly is memory?" To begin with, you should understand that your memory is not a thing that you can point to inside of your brain, nor is it a muscle that somehow gets bigger the more you use it. Instead, memory is the mental capacity to acquire, store, and later retrieve information. It can be argued that memory is central to being who we are. One way to think about how important memory is to your life is to briefly discuss Alzheimer's disease. You may know that this disease afflicts many older individuals, and its primary symptom is the loss of memory. In some cases this memory loss is so severe that a person with Alzheimer's disease cannot recognize or recall family members. From this example, you can clearly see that when memory loss is at this level a person loses their very identity.

Given its importance, it is helpful for you to understand how memory works so that you know what is actually happening when you study. This understanding will hopefully prevent you from taking your memory for granted—there's a lot going on when you try and remember something. Moreover, by understanding how your memory works you might be able to determine ways of studying that improve your memory.

To start, think about memory as involving three steps. First, you have to get information into your memory. This is called acquisition or encoding. A lot of people think this is pretty easy, but your ability to encode something depends on a lot of factors. Many would argue that the most important factor is attention. Your ability to pay attention is limited by the fact that you cannot pay attention to everything; your mental (cognitive) resources are limited. That is why when you need to pay attention to something (e.g., studying a math equation) you need to withdraw attention from other things you might be thinking about (e.g., who you are dating) in order to deal effectively with the math equation. This is called focus. Once you can pay attention to, or focus on the math equation, you can get that information into your memory (i.e., encode it). However, if you keep thinking about the person you are dating at the same time as you are trying to memorize the math equation, you will spend much longer trying to memorize the math equation—if you are able to memorize it at all. Because of the importance of focusing your attention and how it can impact getting information into your memory, you should study in a place where you can focus and not be interrupted or be tempted to think about or look at other things. A piece of advice here: avoid the common area of your college library!

Your ability to acquire information when you study is also impacted by other factors, such as whether you can easily form an image of the item you are trying to remember. Research shows very clearly that items that you can imagine in your mind (what are termed *concrete* items, like a dog) are encoded better than abstract items (e.g., *liberty*). This is why when you study you should try to think of concrete examples to help you remember information. If your instructor talked about issues of *liberty* and *justice*, you might want to visualize the Liberty Bell and the Scales of Justice.

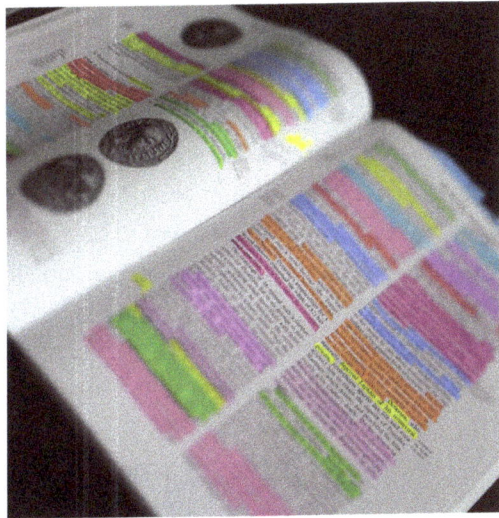

Fig 17.1

Organization also facilitates encoding. As you might suspect, highly organized information is encoded better than unorganized information. This is why when you study you should always try to organize information into meaningful units—what is called *chunking*—like trying to remember all of the metal elements from the periodic table together, rather than the entire table at once. Finally, when you are trying to acquire information, it is critical that you rehearse (i.e., repeat) the information in a certain way. It is not enough to just say things over and over to yourself and think you will remember it. Your greatest chance of remembering something is to give it meaning when you rehearse. For example, imagine you had to remember a phone number (257-2369) that you had no way to write down. You could just keep repeating it over and over throughout the day, but that is not a very efficient strategy. Instead, you would be better off finding some meaning in the numbers, like 2 + 5 = 7 and 2 is right before 3 and then keep adding 3. It may sound like it will not work, but you will be surprised how a little meaning can really improve your ability to acquire information. Also, keep in mind that what may be meaningful to you may not be meaningful to another person. Whatever works for you is what you should use.

Once you encode information, it has to be stored in your memory (i.e., retained) for some period of time if you want to recall it later. There are several ways to discuss how information is stored, but the easiest way to describe storage is to talk about short-term and long-term memory. Short-term memory is also called active memory, because the information that is stored in this type of memory is what you are currently accessing. Think of it this way: when you are studying a specific piece of information, you are conscious of it and you are actively thinking about the information—it is in your short-term memory.

Short-term memory is used all the time, but it has limitations. First, as it name says, it only lasts a relatively short amount of time. Research has shown that if you do not keep rehearsing something like a phone number or an address, you will probably forget it in about 15 seconds. An example will clearly show this. If you need to remember a phone number you would probably start rehearsing it (e.g. repeating it in your mind). But, say someone interrupted you with a question. You would have to stop your rehearsing to talk to the other person. When you tried to recall the phone number after the interruption, the chances are very high that it would be gone from your memory. Another limitation of short-term memory is that its capacity is relatively small. You can only keep about 5–9 items in your short-term memory at any one time. This is fine when you have to remember a phone number or someone's name, but it means that when you are studying for an exam there has to be another type of memory that can store larger amounts of information.

Fig 17.2

This other memory store is, yes you guessed it, long-term memory. Information is trans-ferred from your short-term memory to your long-term memory so you can remember it come exam time. (For those of you interested in biology, one part of your brain that helps makes this happen is called the *hippocampus*.) Once the information gets to long-term memory, you are on your way to great grades. This is because your long-term memory is where you store all of your knowledge. This includes facts about the world (e.g., Napoleon ruled France), how to do things (e.g., ride a bike), and information about all the things that have happened to you in your life (e.g., your date at the senior prom). There is a debate in scientific circles about whether everything in your long-term memory stays there forever or not (i.e., truly permanent, which would mean that any forgetting is a type of retrieval failure), but suffice it to say that when you study you want the information to be ultimately stored in long-term memory and available for retrieval.

Once you have stored information in long-term memory, you might think all is great and you can just take an exam and get an A. Not so fast! Just because you have stored the material in your memory doesn't mean you will remember it on exam day. It is important to consolidate that information in long-term memory (e.g., when you sleep). When you are taking an exam you need to take what you have learned (i.e., consolidated and stored in long-term memory) and bring it to your short-term memory (consciousness) in order to give an answer. Therefore, remembering involves retrieval of information from long-term memory. Two types of re-trieval are recall and recognition. For recall, you must generate the information you need to retrieve—what is the Magna Carta? For recognition, you need to determine that something is familiar—choosing an answer on a multiple-choice exam—you recognize the answer. It would be great if we could retrieve everything at exam time, but as you know from taking exams in the past, it is not so easy. When you cannot retrieve something from your memory, it is called forgetting, and it is what every student who takes an exam is trying to avoid.

QUESTIONS

1. How did you study when you were in high school?

2. What is an example of a time you have made sure to pay attention to something so you would remember it later?

3. Why do you think people take their memory for granted?

4. How will you remember what's key to effective studying? Will this simple diagram help?

Encoding $\longrightarrow$ Storage $\longrightarrow$ Retrieval

FIGURE CREDITS

STUDYING: BASIC CONCEPTS

To help you avoid forgetting, it is important to take what you know about how memory works and follow basic principles of memory improvement. Now some of you may be sitting there saying, "Wait a minute. Why are you going to tell me about principles of memory improvement when all I want is one way to study information so that I do not have to change anything each time I study?" This would be a nice way to deal with all of your coursework, but the problem is that when you study in college, you are faced with a lot of changing factors. For example, there is the nature of the material you are studying. Are you studying for a math exam that involves a lot of equations and problem-solving or for a psychology exam that involves a lot of definitions? There is also the question of how much time you have to study. In some cases you have a lot of time to spread out your studying (called *distributing* your study time, or *spaced practice*), but on other occasions your time is really constrained because of other commitments or exams in other courses. Given this dilemma of an ever-changing studying landscape, it is best to discuss several general principles of memory improvement that can be used for different subjects and in different situations. No one is saying you must use all of them, but if you can use any of them, it will likely help your studying.

FACULTY VOICES:

Avoid the temptation to think that any topic worth learning should emerge translucent just from listening to your instructor or doing the assigned readings. Were the world's intellectual problems only that simple! Study, study, study. You simply have to study!

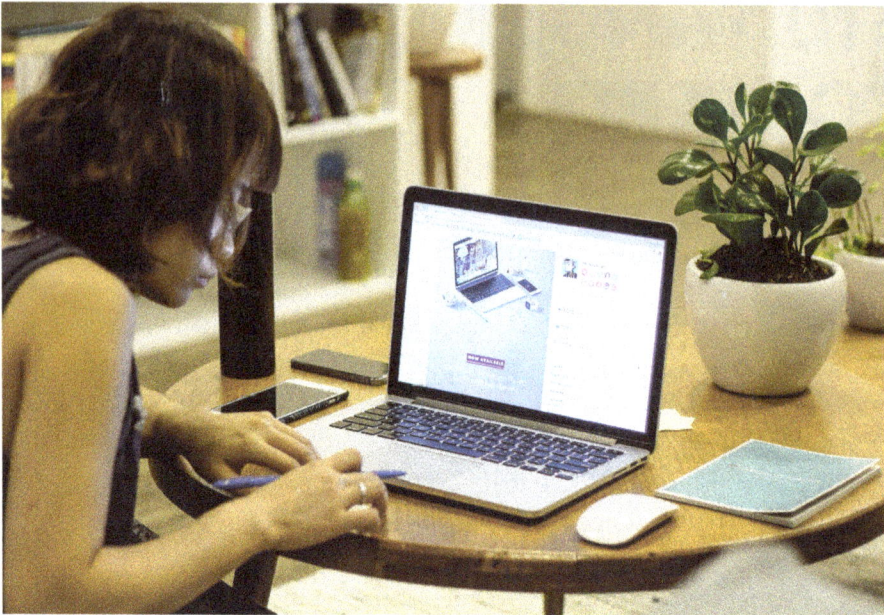

Fig 18.1

PAY ATTENTION

Many experts acknowledge that the most important memory principle is to pay attention. This is because, as stated earlier, if you do not pay attention to what you want to learn that information will never be encoded. For you, the key to paying attention is to make sure that the conditions surrounding your studying (e.g., where you study, when you study) are conducive to paying attention. With this in mind, you should always study in a place that is extremely quiet and has no distracting objects or sounds—you want to focus on the exam material. Does this mean you should not have music playing as you study? For most students, the answer is *yes*, because if you listen at all to the music you take away valuable mental resources from your studying. In addition, you should study at a time when you feel that you are at your peak performance level. Being half asleep when you study will not allow you to focus. Finally, study groups can help you attend to material. Moreover, these groups give you an opportunity to make sure you have learned the material because you often have to teach someone else, and study groups allow you to test each other to practice retrieving information prior to exam day. However, if you study with friends, STUDY! Too often students claim they were studying, but instead they spent more time talking about issues that had nothing to do with exam material.

MAKE THINGS MEANINGFUL

It is best if you can make the material you want to remember meaningful. There are a number of memory strategies (i.e., mnemonics) you can use to give information meaning for encoding. For example, instead of trying to remember a concept like *dog* by repeating it over and over in your mind, you might think about a Golden Retriever that your friend has that chases sticks and brings them back to its owner.

STUDENT VOICES:

… because the easiest way to remember your notes is to remember certain concepts … give them meaning by assigning an example that's meaningful to you … because if you can provide an example, the more likely you are to really retain that.

Other ways to make information meaningful include:

1. using categories (e.g., different breeds of dogs)

2. use related information–take material you already know and associate it to information you want to remember (e.g., stalagmites come up from the ground—the *g* in the word, versus stalactites that hang from the ceiling—the *c* in the word)

3. use rhymes (e.g., *i* before *e* except after *c*)

4. make acronyms that spell something using the first letter of each word you need to remember (e.g., ROY G. BIV—the colors of the visible spectrum—red, orange, yellow, green, blue, indigo and violet)

5. use outrageous imagery that makes a story of what you need to remember

ORGANIZATION

You need to organize the material you want to learn. This can involve looking for patterns in the information. For example, perhaps all the U.S. Presidents you need to learn have a last name starting with the letter "M". Another way to organize material is to chunk it into meaningful groups. An easy example is the following set of letters: FBIDVDCIACBS.

To remember these letters you could try and remember each of the 12 individual letters. Alternatively, you could chunk the letters into meaningful groups (i.e., FBI, DVD, CIA, and CBS) and then only have four chunks of information to remember. Finally, you can create tables to organize your information.

VISUALIZATION

It is useful to visualize information in order to remember it. Research has conclusively shown that the more you can imagine the information by visualizing it, the better you will learn it. This is why concrete words (i.e., words that represent things you can touch and see, like *apple*) are easier to remember than abstract words (i.e., words representing things you cannot touch and see, like *liberty*). However, you can be strategic and turn an abstract word into a concrete word in order to help your memory. For instance, with a word like *liberty* think about the Liberty Bell as a way to help you remember it. Keep in mind that college classes are full of abstract material. Hopefully, your instructor will offer concrete examples to help you visualize abstract concepts. If not, try your best to come up with your own concrete examples.

You can also use mindmapping as a tool for visualization. This technique involves visual imagery, and involves placing a central concept on a piece of paper (or on a computer screen) and then connecting related facts and other concepts to it. It allows you to organize information you want to retain in a creative way (e.g., using a tree with branches instead of Roman numerals). The internet also has computer software for this technique. Drawing diagrams (e.g., Venn diagrams) or pictures can also be helpful.

GET INTERESTED

Try your best to get interested in what you have to remember. You may find this difficult, especially if you are taking a required class for which you have no enthusiasm. Still, avoid getting annoyed about having to take the class. Find something interesting about the material to help motivate you to study. Remember that people generally pay attention to things they are interested in, and if you constantly focus on your irritation at having to study for the course, your focus cannot be on the material and your grade will suffer. You might find information more interesting if you do something like creating PowerPoint slides for yourself with important concepts. Also, you can create some practical use of the concept you want to remember, for example: 1), imagine yourself or someone else using the formula or the idea, going through the steps to solve a real-world problem, 2) see yourself in a classroom teaching the concepts, or 3) thinking about what you would tell your own students about a concept.

IMPORTANCE OF PRACTICE

It is critical that you practice, practice, practice! Make sure that you go over the exam material on multiple occasions. The idea that you would

Fig 18.2

study just once or even a couple of times for an exam is simply ridiculous. Moreover, for some exams you will have a month or more of material—that is a lot of information to learn. You need to start your reviewing as soon as new material is presented and continue your reviewing right up to the start of the exam. This will make the last study session before the exam much easier. Set up a study schedule that includes the dates of your exams, and a time each week (if not each day) to study for a particular exam. Remember, it is very likely that when you have an exam you will have other exams the same week, possibly the same day. And finals week you may have 2–5 exams in a single week! Keep in mind the general principle that distributing your studying over time leads to better memory because it avoids lapses in attention and gives multiple rehearsals (compared to cramming). One other way you can help with practicing is to make a digital recording and listen to it as you drive to class or work.

FEEDBACK

Try to give yourself feedback when you study so you know what you need to study and how well you are doing. This feedback can come from a study group, where you test each other to see what you know and do not know, from rewriting your notes from memory to see where there are gaps that you must review again, from testing using flashcards (discussed in Chapter 19), writing test questions you think the instructor may ask, and taking an exam prepared by another student in your class. Do not put yourself in a position of not knowing whether you have actually learned the material. By testing yourself and getting feedback on your performance, you can accurately gauge whether you need to study more or whether you are remembering all that you had hoped to recall.

AVOID INTERFERENCE

When you study, it is best to try avoiding interference (i.e., when learning one thing disrupts learning something else). There are two things to consider here. The first is related to focusing your attention, as we discussed earlier. When you study, study in a way that allows you to focus on specific material and minimizes the effect of distracting information. Second, you can reduce interference by studying and then going to bed. This way, you give yourself a better chance that the information will be consolidated in your memory with nothing new interfering. Research suggests that activities (e.g., watching television or staying up talking) after studying interferes with encoding and retaining information.

IMPORTANCE OF WHERE YOU STUDY

If you can, try to make where you study similar to where you take the exam. Here's an example to show why this is important. Have you ever taken an exam and experienced the frustration of not being able to recall an item? However, when you get home or go to the room where you study the item comes back to you? Memory can be context dependent, and is most efficient when you encode information (originally learn) and retrieve the information in the same place. What this means is that ideally you would like to study in the same exact seat you are going to take the exam. This is usually not practical, but even studying in the same building as the room you are going to take the exam might help.

DON'T ALWAYS STUDY FROM BEGINNING TO END

If the material allows it, don't just study in order from beginning to end. For some classes this advice will not work since learning material in a certain order is critical (e.g., history is chronological). However, other courses have topics that can really stand by themselves. The problem with studying material only in order is that people are generally very good at recalling the beginning and end of a list (or the first and last topic studied), but not the items in the middle. Your notes are like a list, and if you just study them from beginning to end you run the risk of not learning the information in the middle as well. To avoid this problem, try to study in a way that gives every topic or section an equal chance of being studied in the beginning, middle, and end of a study session. For example if you have three topics on the exam use the following study schedule:

1. Topic 1, Topic 2, Topic 3

2. Topic 2, Topic 3, Topic 1

3. Topic 3, Topic 1, Topic 2

PQRST

As a final thought, organize your studying using a technique that takes into account several of the above memory principles. This technique was developed several decades ago by an education professor and then modified, and is now referred to as the PQRST system. You may not be able to use PQRST all of the time, but it may prove to be effective in some study situations. The PQRST approach involves five actions that make your studying as effective as possible: previewing, questioning, reading, summarizing, and testing. This technique is designed to make the material you are studying "stick" in your memory. Here's some additional detail:

Preview: If you are using a book, skim the chapter, read the introductory paragraph, examine the headings on each page and the summary at the end. The key is to survey the chapter to get a preliminary idea of what the chapter is about, what it contains. If you are going over your notes, you can also look them over to get a general sense of the material.

Question: Start reading the material from your book/notes and as you read, ask yourself such questions as, "Why is this concept important?" "What does the author want me to get from this?" "How does this relate to the prior topic?" "How might this be turned into a test question?"

Reading: As you read you book/notes, try to associate the material with something familiar, something you understand. For instance, in a research methods course you might learn that surveys can be conducted with a whole population or with a sample taken from it. In order to avoid confusing the concepts of *population* and *sample*, you could associate a sample with having a small amount of blood drawn for a test, or taking a sip of coffee to see how hot it is, or sticking your big toe into the tub or pool of water before jumping in. As you read, try to connect the concepts with something you know about. Making notes as you read or highlighting passages in the material are also very useful.

Summarize: In this phase, close your book/cover up your notes and repeat out loud the main points presented in the material. Trying to remember these points helps consolidate your memory. Each time you go over your book/notes, reread everything, review the highlighted portions of your book/notes, or say the things you want to remember, you are strengthening memories, which will aid in recalling the information.

Test: Give your book/notes to a friend, roommate, or study partner and have them ask you questions about the material. Write down what you miss or have forgotten so that you can give those items more attention.

QUESTIONS

1. Which of the memory principles presented have you been using to study?

2. Try to use the memory principles that were presented to think of a mnemonic to remember my name (Jonathan Golding)?

3. Do you ever see yourself using the PQRST process for studying?

FIGURE CREDITS

Figure 18.1: Free-Photos, "Reading Computer," https://pixabay.com/en/office-work-studying-office-working-1149087/.
Figure 18.2: AdinaVoicu, "Studying with Book," https://pixabay.com/en/study-girl-writing-notebook-1231394/.

USING FLASHCARDS TO STUDY FOR EXAMS

Don't assume that flashcards are only for elementary students and skip reading this chapter. They can give you a major boost when preparing for exams. Once you get to college you could be stunned by the amount of studying you will need to do. Almost all of your courses will have some type of exam, and you will need to decide how best to study for each of them. You may think you should study the same way for each exam, but this is probably not the best strategy. Certain subjects and certain types of exams require you to be much more strategic about how you approach studying. For example, it is unlikely that you will study the same way for a math exam that requires you to solve problems and show your work as you would for a multiple-choice psychology exam.

In addition to thinking about how best to study given the subject matter and type of exam, start preparing for exams as soon as you can. Research shows that cramming at the last minute is a bad way to learn. Don't do it! Keep in mind that because of the way college classes are taught, it is likely that you will have more than one exam in the same week or even on the same day. For example, a lot of college classes are set up to give exams every month, so cramming makes it unlikely you can just wait until the night before and have time to study for each exam.

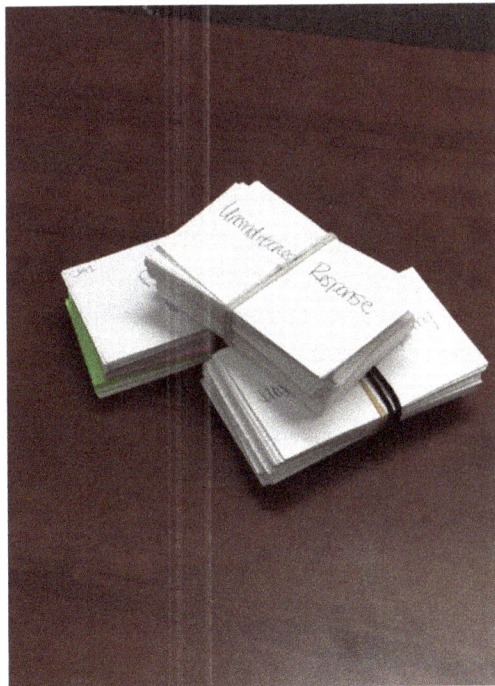

Fig 19.1

In this chapter you will learn about one way to study that works really well for certain types of exams called *objective exams*. On these exams, you select a single correct response from among two or more alternatives, such as a multiple-choice exam or a true-false exam. These types of exams are used in a variety of courses covering many different subjects, especially courses that are considered *survey courses*, which give general information about a subject (e.g., Intro to Sociology). Moreover, objective exams are a relatively easy way to give exams because students take the exam online or in class using a *scantron* or *bubble sheet* (i.e., a sheet where you fill in circles for the correct answers). Thus, they are used a lot for large classes where the number of students typically keeps instructors from giving essay exams, which take a relatively long time to grade.

Our recommended method of studying for objective exams is making flashcards for yourself. Flashcards have an interesting reputation. On the one hand, they are typically viewed as a tool for young children who are learning basic arithmetic. A child reads 2 + 2 on the front of a card and then must come up with the answer of 4. They check their accuracy by looking on the back of the card for the correct answer. On the other hand, research shows that flashcards really have no age limits, and that flashcards are especially useful for college students. If you need to study a large amount of information and you are going to be asked questions with factual answers, as is the case with objective exams, flashcards are an ideal way to study. Flashcards work, whether for learning chemical symbols, psychological terms, or historical events!

To help you understand the effectiveness of flashcards, here is a short description of a research study one of us (Golding) conducted. This study was done a few years ago and published in the journal *Teaching of Psychology*. The study surveyed students in an Intro to Psychology class; there were 415 students in the class and Golding found that 141 students used flashcards to study material for the first three multiple-choice exams. Most of the flashcard users had made the flashcards themselves on 3 × 5 cards instead of using online flashcard sites like *Quizlet*. There has been a big increase in the use of online flashcard sites in just the few years since this research was published, but it is unclear whether it is better to write your own flashcards or type them on a computer. However, research that shows that writing one's notes in class is more effective than typing them on a computer, an argument for writing your own flashcards. The study showed that students who used flashcards on all exams had significantly higher scores overall than those who did not use flashcards on all three exams. This survey also found that about 75% of students used flashcards in at least one of their classes, especially in natural science courses like chemistry and biology.

These are the two points made thus far: 1) flashcards can be very effective, and 2) flashcards are used by a lot of college students. Here is the explanation for why flashcards work. Flashcards make you distribute your studying over an extended time period. This distribution of effort has been shown to lead to better memory compared to studying in one or just a few concentrated bursts (i.e., cramming). Also, flashcards force you to be an active participant in your studying. You don't just sit there and passively read material. Flashcards make you write down (or type) information, think about the best way to remember this information, and constantly test yourself. In this way, you actively process the information you are trying to remember. Next, the very nature of using flashcards puts you in a position of having to manage your study time. When you use flashcards, you must be systematic in how you approach the preparation of the cards, and how you go through the deck of cards to test yourself. There cannot be any randomness in your approach. As you will read later, making and using flashcards requires you to be quite organized, with no room for wasted time.

STUDENT VOICES:

I use usually flashcards for vocabulary terms or key concepts. I wouldn't use them for in-depth questions because it can be hard to remember exactly what it is that you wrote down. For an essay it's better that you work that out as an outline.

Finally, one of the greatest advantages to using flashcards is that it makes your studying more like the objective exams you are preparing for. One concern may be that flashcards do not offer alternative answers like a multiple-choice exam. In the strict sense that is true. But what flashcards do is encourage you to think in terms of small, detailed pieces of information, which is exactly what you need to do when you take multiple-choice exams. You will have a question or statement on one side of a card (e.g., chemical symbol AU?) and then a very specific answer on the other side (GOLD). This is the essence of all objective exams. By studying your cards, you are essentially studying for possible questions that may be on the exam. This symmetry between your flashcards and an exam is likely to show itself in two ways. First, when you take the exam, as you read a question about a specific item, you will remember the flashcard with the information about that material. Of course, remembering the flashcard containing this information will aid in answering the question.

Second, flashcards force you to prepare for any question on the exam. Think of it this way: For any particular objective exam there may be (just as an example) 100 pieces of information your instructor covered in class. Ideally, you will have 100 flashcards to cover this material. You know that the exam will not ask about all 100 pieces of information. Let's say the exam has 30 questions. Your problem, and one that is faced by ALL students taking exams, is that you do not know which 30 of the 100 items will be on the exam. However, since you have flashcards for all 100 items, you should be totally prepared for any question asked. In fact, after the exam there is a high probability that you can go to your deck of 100 flashcards, and be able to pick out the 30 cards that were covered on the exam. Now that is a great study strategy!

With all of this in mind, here is list of nine simple things you should do to prepare your flashcards:

1. Make flashcards after each class, or at least the day of each lecture. It should be pretty obvious why you make them as soon as possible. Memory fades over time, so the sooner you start thinking about your notes and make flashcards, the higher the likelihood that you will memorize the notes as you make the flashcards., and the more time you will have to review those flashcards.

2. Typically, everything in your notes and readings should be on a card. The reason for this gets back to the point raised earlier—you do not know what will be on an exam. Therefore, your best chance of doing well on the exam is to study everything.

3. Your flashcards should be brief. This will make your flashcard questions or statements and answers more like the exam questions and answers. Objective exam questions and answers are usually pretty short. In addition, it is easier to remember the information on a flashcard when it is shorter versus longer. Yes, this will mean that you will likely have more flashcards than if you put a lot of information on a single card. Trust us, having more flashcards is a much better strategy than having fewer flashcards with a ton of information on each. The problem with the latter approach is that each flashcard will *not* correspond to an exam question. In fact, each flashcard will correspond to multiple exam questions. This is not good when the goal is to make your studying more like the exam itself.

Fig 19.2

4. As you write (or type) each flashcard, pay attention and learn the information on the card. Do not just mindlessly write a flashcard. You need to focus and put effort into remembering what the material is about, otherwise all the flashcards will be a waste. The goal is to use the flashcards to help memorize the material.

5. After making flashcards for a particular lecture, shuffle them. If this is your first set of flashcards, just shuffle this one set. If you are adding flashcards to a deck you

already started, shuffle all of the flashcards together. The reason for shuffling is to place your cards in random order—which is very likely the way your objective exam will present questions. By shuffling the cards, you are again making your studying more like taking the exam.

6. Test yourself using the flashcards right after you make them. It is not enough to just make the cards, you need to test yourself to determine what you know and what you do not know; feedback is critical to using flashcards.

7. As you study, make a pile for the flashcards you know (the *Know* pile) and a pile for the flashcards you don't know (the *Don't Know* pile). Hopefully, your deck of *Know* flashcards will be much higher than the deck of *Don't Know* flashcards.

8. Go back over the *Don't Know* pile until you can answer each flashcard correctly. One of the keys to using flashcards is efficiency. In this case, efficiency is tied to making sure you learn the information you did not initially get correct. The cards you already know do not need additional time at this moment—you'll study them again the next time you add flashcards.

9. Continue to make new flashcards after each lecture, add them to your old flashcards, shuffle the deck, and then test yourself as before. This leads to a continuous flow of testing and retesting. By the time you take the exam, you will have studied all of the material a number of times, and you will know the material way better than someone who waited to study until just before the exam.

If you follow these steps, you will find that using flashcards really helps you in courses that lend themselves to this type of study strategy. Try using flashcards. You'll be surprised at how much they can improve your test scores.

QUESTIONS

1. What are some classes you are taking where it would be effective to use flashcards?

2. Have you ever gone online to check out sites that let you make flashcards (e.g., Quizlet)?

3. Were you surprised to read about the effectiveness of flashcards? Why?

FIGURE CREDITS

PREPARING TO TAKE EXAMS IN COLLEGE

In most colleges, you will encounter exams at least at the midpoint of the academic term (midterms) and usually at the end of the term (finals). Usually, although it could vary on your particular campus, the last week of the academic term is set aside just for taking exams. The timing of final exams is often determined by a process designed to rotate the days and times when instructors conduct them. Although you will know at the beginning of the semester when your exams are scheduled, you generally won't have that information for future semesters. No one really worries about this. The rotation of exam days and times is beyond your control (kind of like selecting a winning lottery ticket). This means that during finals week, you might have three exams the first day or none at all. Your exams might be nicely spaced (e.g., one per day) or be all bunched up together.

In this chapter, we discuss ways to prepare for your exams before the actual test date. There are two main strategies: anticipating the content of exam questions, and what you can do to prepare for exams.

PROFESSORS AS A SOURCE OF EXAM QUESTIONS

Because your professors are educators, it is safe to assume that they will be giving numerous reminders or hints about what is important to know. Pay attention to the orchestration of what happens in class: What items are written on the board? What vocabulary items or concepts appear on PowerPoint slides? What is the purpose behind having you complete the various assignments? As educators, professors want you to learn and they especially want you to learn the main principles, rules, theories, etc. that they lecture or have you read about. These reminders occur in the first weeks of the semester as well as throughout the whole semester and are particularly important when you prepare for *cumulative* exams. If your final exam is cumulative, this means that all material prior to the exam is covered. It may mean that you can expect questions on that exam to be similar to those the instructor asked on earlier exams and quizzes. However, it makes sense to ask about the format of the exam. While it is highly likely that multiple-choice questions will generally be the rule in large lecture classes, in smaller classes the instructor may choose from a number of differ types of exam formats (see Chapter 23). That's why you need to ask. Be prepared. Don't be surprised.

Once you are clear on the exam format, identify possible exam questions this way: What did the instructor spend the most time talking about during each lecture? Look at your lecture notes and consider using a highlighter to identify the main theme or themes from each session. Also, look to see if the amount of coverage in the instructor's PowerPoint slides (if they were posted) corresponds with your notes. Make sure you can answer these questions:

- What was the focus of each assignment you completed? How could each topic be asked about as an exam question?

- What were you quizzed on? Could these items be slightly modified and appear again?

- Make a list of the items that were covered or mentioned enough times to make the list as *important* or *could be important*. At a minimum, walk into the exam knowing these items and being able to apply them appropriately.

Thinking about your course and the instructor's lectures analytically will help you see that exam questions usually flow from what you were expected to learn by reading, attending to the lectures, doing assignments, and so forth. Sometimes the course syllabus lists objectives, which are also a good indication of what you are expected to learn.

The bulk of any exam will not cover cryptic or esoteric material hidden away in a footnote or under the caption of a table. That is, the vast majority of the exam should be over material that 1) you were assigned to read, 2) the instructor lectured about, 3) students discussed or had assignments about, or 4) appeared in a study guide prepared by the instructor or the TA. Where you see an alignment of two, three, or four of these course components, then the likelihood is higher that material is important enough to be covered in an exam.

Additional information about what might appear on an exam can come from any review session conducted by the professor or his/her TA, and any old exams made available by the professor or found in the library or online.

> **FACULTY VOICES:**
> *Exams in college are often focused more on applying and integrating your knowledge, rather than rote memorization.*

WHAT STUDENTS CAN DO TO PREPARE FOR EXAMS

You may not realize it, but there are a lot of things you can do to prepare yourself for even a really tough exam. However, they all depend on giving yourself enough time to take advantage of these tips. Let's say that the first exam sent you a message, and that you now realize you can't take a chance on inadequately preparing. Let's further assume that you have four or five weeks to employ some effective strategies to prepare for exams. Here's what you can do:

- In some courses (e.g., math) that are incremental and build sequentially, if you miss key content early (e.g., sickness, death in the family) or you don't understand *any* portions of the course content (e.g., you are not doing well on quizzes or assignments), meet with the TA or the instructor to become more competent in those areas. As we have suggested before, you have no reason to fear making an appointment with the TA or instructor. Your questions could inform them that possibly other students need help too. (Assuming that for every student who asks for help there could be 5 to 10 students who need help but don't ask.)

- Divide the material to be on the exam into thirds: the material that you know well, the material you mostly know but need to review, and the material that you don't know. Spend more of your study time on the material you don't know, then what you need to review, and the least time on what you know well.

- Develop a study plan that budgets an adequate amount for studying and your other responsibilities. If you have too little time to devote to studying, try to reduce your other obligations. Cut back on your work or volunteer hours if possible. Inform your parents or significant others away from campus that you won't be coming home or visiting before a major exam or during the last two weeks of the semester.

- Indicate on your calendar or day planner the due dates of any course projects, assignments, or papers that may occur at the same time as scheduled exams. Complete these early if possible to free up more time for studying.

- See if your textbook publisher has provided study questions, outlines, or resources to aid studying. Many textbooks list questions at the end of each chapter. Don't overlook these. The instructor could draw from these questions or slightly revise them for an exam. If no resources are available from the textbook publisher, then look online for explanations or examples that other instructors may have posted.

- Start reviewing for the exam early. Begin by reviewing your class notes, noting things you need to remember or look up. Actually look them up and write these items down.

Fig 20.1

- If you are a terrible note taker or lack confidence in your ability to do well on exams, find a study partner or group.

- Review the previous chapter in this book (Chapter 18) about how to study and pay special attention to the fact that you must not distract yourself when studying. As one website said, you must "unplug, disconnect." Remember also, you must encode the material, practice it, and self-test.

A DAY OR TWO BEFORE THE EXAM

- Don't pull an all-nighter. Don't assume you can get by with 2–3 hours of sleep and do just as well as if you had 6–8 hours. You can't. Your brain needs rest to consolidate the information you have been trying to learn.

- Check out the exam location if it is in a different building or location. Be sure of where you are going. Don't make the mistake of going to the wrong place.

- Make a list of things you need to bring to the exam (e.g., ID, calculator, etc.)

THE DAY OF THE EXAM

- Eat breakfast in order to avoid being distracted by an empty stomach.

- Give yourself plenty of time to get ready and have a quick review.

- When you receive the exam, give it a quick look so that you will know the number of questions, the format, types of questions, etc.

- Don't scare yourself and panic if you don't know the answer to the first question or two. Go forward but come back to the question(s) that stumps you later.

- Watch your time to make sure you don't spend too much time on any one question.

- Read the instructions. Make sure you understand what is being asked and how much each question counts.

- Keep your eyes on your own paper so that you aren't accused of trying to cheat.

- If there are short answer questions, write a complete sentence or even sentences rather then answering in a word or two. Look at the space allocated for the answer. The instructor may be looking for a more full explanation or rationale for the response than you are planning to give.

- Don't be in a hurry to leave. Double check your answers, take a stab at any questions you don't know. Don't leave any questions blank.

Lastly, once you see your midterm or final grades, make a mental note about the courses where you performed best and where you didn't do so well. Reflect on your own efforts and the strategies you used. This reflection may give you good information for your next exams, next semester and beyond.

ONLINE EXAMS

Increasingly, faculty teach more online and hybrid (combination of face-to-face meetings along with online assignments and content) courses. These may allow students to take courses electronically on their laptops at home or in large proctored rooms. Electronic exams always pose something of a dilemma for the faculty member—especially when students take them at home or outside of the classroom. This is because faculty members have much less control of the setting and students

Fig 20.2

could cheat, for instance, by having books and reference papers nearby, or even having a classmate take the test for them. Accordingly, faculty try to create exams that while being fair, could have some different rules attached to them.

For instance, you may have to upload a copy of your college/university ID picture and have your laptop's camera focused on you the whole time you are taking the exam. Or the instructor may decide to give you less time than with a face-to-face exam to submit a response. Some course management systems (like Canvas) allow the instructor to present only one question at a time, and in a random order, so that two students sitting side by side cannot see the same question at the same time. You might be allowed to go forward only to unanswered questions and not allowed to go back and change responses to questions you have already answered.

If you are required to take an online exam, be sure that your computer doesn't have any annoying problems like being slow or needing updates. Close all programs and tabs except the one you need for the exam. Do not read or answer email during the exam, as that could get you charged with cheating. Do not refer to your cell phone unless you need to be available to receive a call from work or home, or the instructor gives you permission to answer your phone if it rings. Go into the exam prepared!

QUESTIONS

1. Is it easy or difficult for you to plan? Explain.

2. As you think about your own personal approach to preparing for exams, are there additional bullet points you would add to the tips above? What would they be?

3. Do you find it easy to talk to professors and TAs? Why or why not? What would make it easier to talk to them?

FIGURE CREDITS

Figure 20.1: videorevive, "Woman Studying," https://pixabay.com/en/girl-school-university-education-476977/.
Figure 20.2: StockSnap, "Woman Studying," https://pixabay.com/en/laptop-apple-macbook-computer-2561018/.

EXAM QUESTION TYPES: WHAT YOU NEED TO KNOW

Very few students going to college look forward to taking exams. Yet, we all know exams are a fact of college life. Just like the professors who administer them, exams vary in appearance, in the number of questions, in their difficulty level, and in the types of questions. While we can't help you with some of these dimensions along which exams differ, we can explain diverse exam formats and offer some suggestions for dealing with different types of questions.

To begin, there are seven types of assessment questions: 1) multiple choice, 2) true/false, 3) matching, 4) short answer, 5) essay, 6) fill-in-the-blank, and 7) computational. Each of these will be discussed in turn. But first, remember this tip: whenever you are presented with an exam, immediately look through it to see what type of questions are asked and how many of each type there are. This will help you to allocate your time so that you don't spend too much on any one item and run out of time on the others.

MULTIPLE CHOICE QUESTIONS

During your first year in college you will very likely experience large lecture classes, and the exam format used to assess your learning in those courses will most often be multiple-choice (also known humorously as "multiple-guess") questions. Because of the prominence of multiple-choice exams, we devote a whole chapter to them (Chapter 22). Thus, this chapter focuses on the other six types of exam questions.

TRUE/FALSE QUESTIONS

True/false items are good for checking retention of facts. They are similar to multiple-choice questions, but with only two alternatives. Many instructors like these types of questions because they don't take long to construct and are quick to score. Although students may believe differently, most instructors never set out to develop trick true/false questions that hinge on some frivolous piece of knowledge. Generally, instructors try to develop questions around key concepts where the answer would be apparent to students who read the course material. For instance, let's say students are assigned to read a passage about life in the United States during World War II that discussed, among other things, the rationing of commodities (like sugar and gas) during that time period. An instructor might ask, "True or False: During World War II, in the United States, both sugar and gas were rationed." The argument for the exam item is that food items made with sugar are important to most people—and can you imagine not being able to get all the gas you might want or need? It sounds too preposterous that both gas and sugar would be rationed. Consequently, students who haven't read the article would likely indicate *False*. Students who read the material should get it right.

This type of item could encourage guessing. Nonetheless, you will likely encounter true/false items on exams.

TIPS FOR ANSWERING TRUE/FALSE QUESTIONS

1. Read the entire statement carefully; don't jump too early to a choice. Look for any qualifiers like *always*, *never*, and *every* that indicate there are no exceptions and the statement must be true all of the time. The presence of these qualifiers usually indicate that the statement is false.

2. Qualifiers like usually, typically, and generally, often suggest the statement is true.

3. If any part of the statement is incorrect or false, the answer must be False. If the statement contains both true and false components, it cannot be True.

Fig 21.1

MATCHING QUESTIONS

These exam items typically require you to recognize a term in one column with a short definition or example in another column. Sometimes you draw lines to connect the pairs, but other times you respond with a number or letter for the corresponding match.

TIPS FOR ANSWERING MATCHING QUESTIONS

1. Answer the items you are most sure of first.

2. Use a process of elimination and try to recall any associations that allow you to link one of the terms or examples with something in the other column.

3. Read the instructions carefully to make sure that there is only one match allowed per item (as opposed to two or more terms corresponding to one concept).

SHORT-ANSWER QUESTIONS

Even when an exam is primarily multiple choice, often there is a sprinkling of short-answer questions. Unless you are in a very small class, it is unlikely that you would ever see an important exam composed entirely of short-answer questions. From an instructor's viewpoint, they are easier to grade than essay questions, but can still slow down the grading process, especially when students respond in longhand and their penmanship is difficult to decipher. This type of exam item allows students the hope of getting partial credit if their response isn't totally correct, depending upon the instructor and the exam.

There are several varieties of short-answer questions. Essentially, you could be asked to: provide a definition; explain a concept, theory, or relationship; describe an example; compare and contrast; solve a problem or calculate an answer; list steps; or create a graph, diagram, or figure. It is incumbent on you to ask the instructor before the exam what type of questions will be asked. In some classes, you might encounter more than one type of short-answer question.

TIPS FOR ANSWERING SHORT-ANSWER QUESTIONS

1. Prepare for this type of exam question by focusing on key terms, definitions, dates, events, and concepts—some of the same material that would be on your flashcards.

2. If you are asked to provide a definition (e.g., independent variable) then explain the term; don't suggest an example or talk around the issue by saying what the concept resembles. If you are asked to provide an example, don't lapse into defining the term or concept. Explanation questions may require you to interpret a concept for your reader (the instructor or TA), as if they don't know what you know. It might help to think about steps, stages, or stimulus-response causation for your explanation. Similarly, if asked to compare and contrast, be sure to do both parts (i.e., compare=similarities and contrast=differences) and address the specific concept being asked about.

3. Don't take the time to rewrite or restate the question. Take a moment to plan what you want to say before starting to write.

4. Don't answer with a single word or two. Observe how much space the question allows and try to give an adequate response using most of the space and complete sentences. However, if asked to list steps, complete sentences may not be needed.

5. With computation problems, show your formulae or methodology. Show each step in working out the solution. If diagraming or graphing, label all parts, complete with headings.

6. You may want to leave a blank line or two in case you think of something you want to add and have time to come back to this item.

ESSAY QUESTIONS

Students either love or hate this type of exam question. Students who can organize their thoughts quickly and write well probably do the best with them. Essay questions offer students the greatest opportunity to showcase what they know. Students who don't do well on essay questions are those who are less prepared and need the prompting of possible responses (e. g. multiple choice items) to recall key elements for their essay, and students who don't write well or take longer to ponder the correct approach for writing down their thoughts.

An exam composed entirely of essay questions is more likely to occur in a philosophy, or English literature course and small classes where students are expected to develop original thought or reflection and show competence in writing. However, many college instructors include a single essay question with other question types on an exam. As you can imagine, it takes considerably longer to grade essay answers and from a teacher's perspective, essays are not as objective as other exam items. Nonetheless, it is usually obvious when students know what they are talking about and when they don't. Teachers find it much harder to grade essays in the "gray middle" where students ramble and aren't sure what's important, so they throw unrelated material into their responses—"everything but the kitchen sink"—in an effort to get partial credit. Add to that the problem of incomprehensible student handwriting and you can see why many instructors minimize their use of essay exams.

TIPS FOR ANSWERING ESSAY QUESTIONS

1. Prepare for essay questions by thinking about the topics covered in class and assigned readings. Jot down potential exam questions and take the time to write out or list the points you would make in an answer. Do this without referring to your notes or textbook. Then check to see if you left out anything important.

2. During the exam, read the questions slowly to make sure you know what you are being asked to do.

3. Take a moment to organize your thoughts before you start writing. On a scrap sheet of paper, or on the back of a page or margin of the paper, list the important points you want to make. Think about the order they should come in.

4. Consider this like any other writing assignment you might have outside of class. Set the stage for your response with an opening paragraph (an overview) and provide some context or background for the thesis or response you are going to give. Each essential point you make should be its own paragraph. Use complete sentences.

5. Where possible, give specific examples to show relationships or to support your explanation. Instructors will be looking for facts and details, and may use a rubric (i.e., a scoring guide). Having worked out the correct answer ahead of time, the instructor will know that there are certain points that students ought to mention. For full credit, your response would need to address all of those points. For example, if there are five possible points to make and you mention four, you would get 80% correct for that essay question.

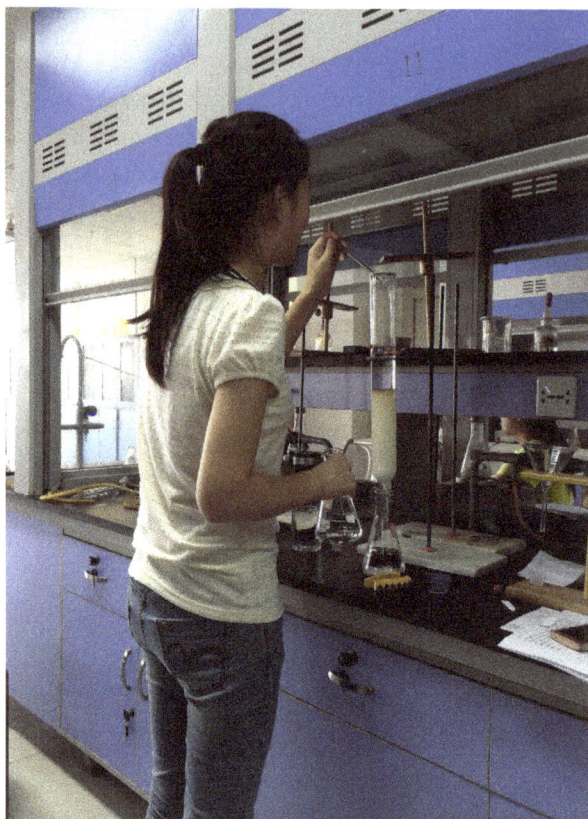

Fig 21.2

6.   Check to make sure you respond to everything the question asked, then summarize your response in a concluding paragraph.

7.   Budget your time. Don't run over the amount of time allocated to answer the question.

8.   If you are running out of time, write your answer using bullet points to list your key ideas instead of full sentences. Otherwise, use full sentences.

FILL-IN-THE-BLANK QUESTIONS

One doesn't see this format a great deal in college classrooms, however, some instructors may use it. Many students are familiar with its presentation as an incomplete statement—a sentence with a hole or blank spot in it. Fill-in-the-blank items require you to recall memorized facts. You will be inundated with more facts in college classes than you are used to from high school. Consequently, students can have a difficult time knowing which facts are important enough to commit to memory and which are just trivia. When students struggle with these exam items, it could be because they underprepared. However, students and faculty can have different perspectives on the appropriate key word to fill in the blank. To prepare for these types of items, your best offense is to pay special attention to key words in your text and lectures, especially when the instructor or the book goes to the trouble of providing a definition of a concept. Flashcards could be a good way to study for this type of question.

TIPS FOR ANSWERING FILL-IN-THE-BLANK QUESTIONS

1. See if the question itself provides any clues. Can you match any parts of the sentence with a key word or phrase you have studied?

2. If there are spaced intervals to indicate the number of words required (e.g., three separate blanks = three words), this might suggest the possible answer.

3. Be sure to read the instructions. Could a long blank indicate more than one word? If there are no instructions, be bold and hold your hand up and ask for clarification from the instructor or TA.

COMPUTATIONAL QUESTIONS

In certain types of classes (e.g., math, physics, chemistry), students can expect computational questions on exams. The exam questions will likely mirror homework assignments. Before beginning to study for this type of question, determine from your instructor or TA if you can bring in, say, on an index card, any formulae or equations that will be needed. If not allowed, then a key to your success will be memorizing the elements needed to calculate solutions. Also check to see if students may bring calculators.

TIPS FOR ANSWERING COMPUTATIONAL QUESTIONS

1. Quickly look through the exam and answer the easiest questions first.

2. Read the questions carefully and fully understand what they are asking. Don't rush to start solving unless you are certain of what you need to calculate or demonstrate.

3. Show all of your work. Be neat, and use labels, headings, or captions where needed.

4. Keep track of the time remaining and the questions still to be answered. Don't deprive yourself of a good grade by spending most of your time trying to solve one or two questions and running out of time for all the rest.

FINAL TIPS REGARDLESS OF EXAM QUESTION FORMAT

1. Never leave a question blank. Even with a fill-in-the-blank question, you might get partial credit if you come up with a synonym or part of a phrase. The only exception to this tip is if you are going to be penalized for wrong answers; then you can leave questions blank.

2. When an answer doesn't come to you immediately, mark the question, go on to other questions, and if there is time, go back to the marked questions.

3. Be sure to read instructions and questions completely and to answer all parts of the questions.

4. Particularly with short answer questions, never assume that you can answer them with a one or two word response. Tailor the length of your response to close to the amount of space allocated for it.

5. Try to anticipate the questions that the instructor will ask on the exam; have a study buddy develop an exam on the material for you.

6. When memorization is needed, practice!

QUESTIONS

1. What type of exam formats do you expect to encounter in the major you are planning for college?

2. Reflect on the exam format that gives you the most difficulty. What can you do to handle that format more confidently in the future?

3. How difficult is it for you to memorize material that may be on an exam?

4. What have you learned thus far in this book about improving your memory while studying?

TAKING MULTIPLE-CHOICE EXAMS

In college, for better or worse, you will likely deal with two things you need to be prepared for: large classes and multiple-choice exams. Large classes are partly a function of the fact that there are simply not enough faculty to teach small classes. Just to be *large* is a relative term. That is, even if you are at a relatively small college there are bound to be classes that are larger than the typical class. So, while a large university may have courses with enrollments of 500 students, a large course at a small college may be an enrollment of 100. The point is, a large class is very different than a small class. Courses with large enrollments are used to teach *survey courses*. These are introductory cours- es designed to give you broad coverage of a subject (e.g., Introduction to Psychology). Because survey courses cover a lot of information, these courses

Fig 22.1

use a lecture format where instructors present information to the class, instead of a seminar format where the class and instructor interact a great deal as they discuss material.

With large classes come multiple-choice exams. These exams are sometimes referred to as *objective* exams because there is only one answer alternative that is correct. Another type of question on objective exam is true-false questions. The reasons why large classes use multiple-choice exams are pretty simple. While it is true that multiple-choice exams are ideal for asking questions about the vast amount of information you learn in a survey course, what really seems to drive the use of these exams is that they make evaluating students more time-efficient, and the grading is more consistent because subjectivity in grading does not come into play. With regard to the former, can you imagine how long it would take an instructor (even with the assistance of TAs) to read and grade 500 essay exams, each of which had 5 questions? Easily many hours, if not days. Compare this to giving a 50-question multiple-choice exam that is scored by a computer-run scanning machine in a matter of minutes! With regard to the absence of subjectivity, remember that multiple-choice exams have only one correct response. Therefore, instructors do not have to worry about following a scoring rubric, or whether they scored each answer in exactly the same way.

Given that the use of multiple-choice exams is not ending any time soon, it is important on exam days that you know certain test-taking strategies. You will either take the exam online or in your classroom as a paper-and-pencil exam. If your exam is online, you will mark the answer on the computer screen. Online questions are usually presented in a random order, and every classmate sees a different order. Also, some instructors allow all of the questions to appear at once, so you can easily scroll back and forth between questions, but other instructors only let you see one question at a time. When one question at a time is presented, it is quite a pain to go back and check answers.

If the multiple-choice exam is given in a classroom as a paper-and-pencil exam, you will typically bring or be given a *bubble-sheet* or a *scantron* sheet to mark your answers, and an exam booklet with the exam questions. A machine scans and scores the answer sheets. You "bubble in" (fill in) the circles using a pencil to mark your name and other identifying information on the answer sheet. It is extremely rare for instructors to have you mark answers directly in the exam booklet, because it would take much more time to go through each page to grade the exam. Also, some instructors let you keep the exam booklet, but others require you to turn it in with your scantron sheet. One reason instructors might not want to let you keep the exam booklet is that it takes a long time to construct a valid exam, and they do not want all of their questions and answers available across campus, knowing that next semester they will have to construct a brand new exam.

When you first receive a multiple-choice exam, give it a quick look over and make sure to read the instructions to be sure you understand exactly what you are required to do as you take the exam. You want to know how many questions are on the exam because that tells you how much each question is worth (e.g., 50 questions = two points per question) and how to time yourself as you take the exam. Some students like to quickly calculate the maximum amount of time they can spend on each question. You must realize that timing is critical when you take a multiple-choice exam. If you have 50 questions to answer and it is a 50-minute exam, you have one minute per question. Thus, you cannot take very long per question.

Your instructor may not tell you very much about the exam before you take it. However, hopefully you will already know important things like the number of questions, and how many alternatives (response choices) there are for each question. The more alternative choices, the more difficult it is to answer the question. If there are four alternatives you have a 25% chance of being correct, if you completely guess. As the number of alternatives increases, your chance of guessing correctly decreases (e.g., five alternatives = 20% likelihood of being correct). Finally, prior to the exam your instructor may give you practice questions or let you look at old exams so to give you a feel for how questions will be asked and what alternatives might look like. This can be important, because multiple-choice questions and alternative answers can be long or short, and the correct answer to a question can include a single alternative, multiple alternatives (e.g., *a and b*), *all of the above*, or (the dreaded) *none of the above*.

A second strategy you can use when taking a multiple-choice exam can only be used if you are able to skip questions in order to answer them later. This strategy involves answering all of the easier questions first. This lets you be sure you will not miss out answering the easier questions, because you spent too long on the harder questions. In addition, by dealing with the easier questions first you allow yourself to focus solely on the harder questions. If you read a question that you consider hard, skip it and move on to the next question. To help locate the hard questions in the exam booklet later, make a mark in the booklet next to each question you skip. It is best not to make any marks on your scantron sheet, because the machine that scans them is sensitive and you would never want a reminder mark to be read by the scanner as an answer. If you mark the exam booklet for skipped questions, make sure you do not fill in the circle on the scantron sheet for the skipped question—this is a very easy mistake to make!

STUDENT VOICES:

With multiple-choice exams it's important not to get caught up on one question if you don't know the answer.

Third, if you can, try to think of the answer or multiple answers to a question immediately after reading it, before reading any of the possible alternatives. In fact, you might want to cover all of the answers with your hand as you are reading the question. Then, with the answer(s) in your mind, look at the response choices and see whether there is a match or not.

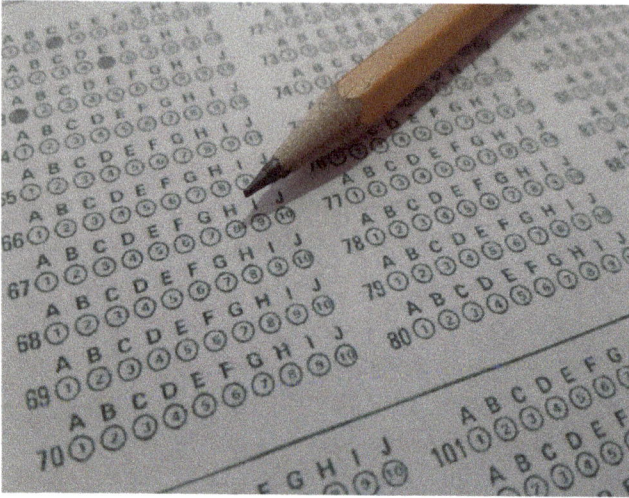

Fig 22.2

This strategy makes alternatives like *all of the above, a and b* or *none of the above* easier to select, because all you are doing is checking for the match between what you came up with and what is on the exam. For example, say you read a question and come up with two possible answers (*reinforcement* and *reward*). Then you look at the alternatives. If alternative *a* is *reward"* and no alternative says *reinforcement,* you choose *a.* As a second example, if you read a question and come up with two possible answers (*punishment* and *pain*) you look for these two words. If alternative *a* says *punishment* and alternative *b* says *pain* you then look to see if there is an alternative that says "*a and b.*" Finally, if you come up with an answer in your head that did not match any of the alternatives provided, you know the correct answer must be *none of the above.*

Besides helping you select the correct alternative, another reason for covering up the alternatives is that sometimes seeing an answer pushes you to select it too quickly because it looks or sounds correct. For example, in class you might have heard the term *operant conditioning* but on the exam you see the term *operatic conditioning.* These are not the same thing, but they look similar. If you quickly looked at the answer *operatic conditioning* you might select it without giving it enough thought. By covering up the answers you force yourself to really think about and generate the correct answers and not be *tricked* into picking an incorrect alternative.

Fourth, if you feel that covering up the answers will not work for you, another approach you can take is strategic elimination. Read the question and then go through each alternative one at a time to see whether that alternative is correct or not. This strategy helps you see if there is more than one correct alternative (an answer like *a and b* or *all of the above*), or if no alternatives are correct (the answer *none of the above*). However, sometimes this elimination strategy leads you to think that there are two reasonable choices, and there is no alternative that allows for both. Your best hope at that point is that you know the material well enough to select the correct alternative.

Fifth, in most cases you will not penalized for guessing on multiple-choice exams, so you should feel free to go for it. It is often the case that if you have to guess, you can make educated guesses that are not just random stabs at an answer. Your can use these tips for educated guesses:

1. Answers with absolute words (e.g., *all*, *never*) are usually incorrect.

2. Answers with qualifiers (e.g., *some*, *generally*) are usually correct.

3. Correct answers sometimes repeat one or more of the terms in the question.

4. Partly true and partly false answers are incorrect.

5. If two answers are opposites, one of the answers is likely correct.

6. Answers with unfamiliar terms tend to be incorrect.

7. If two answers mean almost the same thing and there is no alternative like *a* and *b*, both are probably incorrect.

8. Just because an answer looks correct, it doesn't mean it is correct (e.g., *operatic* is not the same as *operational*).

9. Use only what you learned in lecture and your required reading(s) when answering; avoid using information from outside of the class.

10. Longer answers have a tendency to be correct because the instructor was trying to be precise.

If you cannot make an educated guess or you do not have time to read the questions remaining, you might want to select the same alternative for each question you cannot answer. That is, choose *a* for each of these questions. This strategy is based on the fact that each alternative has about the same random likelihood of being correct, assuming that your instructor was not purposely choosing certain alternatives to occur more often than others. Don't leave questions blank.

Sixth, it is extremely important that you review your answers. There is a myth that you should never change the first answer that you mark on your scantron. However, research conclusively shows that changing answers will not lead to significantly more incorrect answers. In fact, changing answers can lead to more correct responses. So don't immediately rush out of the classroom once you complete the exam. If you have time left, use it to your advantage by checking your answers. One thing you might want to do if the time you have left is limited is to just look back over the questions you had designated as difficult.

> **FACULTY VOICES:**
>
> *When taking a multiple-choice exam, make sure to read the question carefully and then read all of your choices. Sometimes the question asks you to pick the answer that is not correct. Make sure you realize what the question is asking for. As I have found in writing these types of exams, one or even two choices will be easy to discard as incorrect. Then based on what you covered in class, you should be able to pick out the correct answer. Also if there is a study guide, use the study guide! Take the time to answer all of the questions in the study guide and that will definitely help you with a multiple-choice exam.*

Finally, as you go through the exam, don't try to guess what the instructor had in mind when he or she made up the exam. Just because an a answer hasn't appeared for a while doesn't mean that one is about to appear. Overthinking in this way will likely lead to errors. Your time is better spent just answering the questions than trying to figure out what your instructor was thinking when arranging the order of the correct responses.

QUESTIONS

1. In the past, have you taken multiple-choice exams with no real strategy? Why?

2. How do you typically deal with hard questions on a multiple-choice exam? Do you simply answer them in order or skip them and answer them after you have dealt with easier questions?

3. Do you like multiple-choice exams? Why?

FIGURE CREDITS

Figure 22.1: anneileino, "Large Classroom," https://pixabay.com/en/the-audience-the-public-lecture-1254036/.
Figure 22.2: lecroitg, "Scantron," https://pixabay.com/en/test-testing-bubble-form-test-form-986935/.

THE LIBRARY IS YOUR FRIEND

Imagine that you are about to begin your college career. You have moved into your residence hall, attended campus orientation sessions, met with your advisor, familiarized yourself with your campus's layout, and located all of your classrooms. Now you have a day free before classes begin. If there is one building that you should explore to get a head start on your academic success, which building would that be? If your answer is campus library, then we are on the same page!

Fig 23.1

You are no doubt familiar with libraries. Your high school probably had at least a small library, and you may have had a public library in your community. Depending on the size of your hometown, the public library might have been a large structure comparable in size to your campus library. Although similar in structure, public and campus libraries function differently. In particular, a campus library houses a large variety of resources that are critical to your undergraduate education. It behooves you to get to know this critical resource well as quickly as you can.

There is much more to be found in the campus library than books, although you will, indeed, find books there. Despite the growth in electronic publishing that now offers online versions of books, journals, magazines, newspapers, and even textbooks, you will nonetheless find the need for books and services found in your campus library. So go to that building and explore it thoroughly. Visit every floor and open space, and get familiar with what the library contains, where services are located, and get to know the people who work there and learn what they do.

Much of the value in your campus library relates to the modern concept of *information literacy*, which is a set of skills that describe how a person interacts effectively with information. Information literate people can recognize when they need information and have the ability to find the right information, evaluate it, and use it effectively. *Information literacy* skills include the ability to navigate library resources, evaluate information for bias and relevancy, communicate the results of your research effectively, and provide attribution for the information sources you use. A librarian may teach information literacy skills in distinct class sessions, or your professor may incorporate learning the skills into a research assignment. These skills are essential for any informed citizen and are relevant to you regardless of your major. Understanding how to find and use information will benefit you throughout your college career, and your employers will expect you to bring those skills to the work place, regardless of profession.

Fig 23.2

To further prepare you to take advantage of the campus library, which at large universities usually consists of a system of buildings, or rooms within buildings spread across campus, use the maps and descriptive materials that the campus library itself makes available to students. These materials outline the kinds of resources available and where to find them. This information is also typically found online. Click on the campus library link on your institution's web site and examine the site thoroughly. If your campus library offers tours and information sessions, take advantage. Do not wait until one of your teachers sends you to the library with an explicit assignment. Get ahead of the game!

One of the most valuable resources found in a campus library is its people. Modern librarians function as information specialists. They are specially trained to know all of the information resources available, both in traditional print format and in electronic versions. They are also experts in the skills needed to use those materials. A common location within the campus library to find a librarian is the *reference desk*, where you are likely to find a *reference librarian* available to offer assistance and answer questions about information resources and about the library itself.

FACULTY VOICES:

The library has, or can get, all the resources you need to write the research papers you will have to complete during your college career. An academic library can be difficult to navigate at first, so the library has humans (librarians!) who can help you use thee resources effectively. If you take time to learn how to use the library you will save time and heartache, write better papers, get better grades, and develop skills that will serve you well after you graduate.

There are some specific resources to look for as well. One invaluable resource is the library's hard copy offerings and online versions of reference materials. Today we think of using Google or other search engines to find online resources, but a search engine will not necessarily give you access to certain resources provided by the library. For example, there are highly specific, searchable references that you will need for courses that require you to conduct background research as part of a project or in order to write a research paper. Librarians can help you identify these resources, many of which are domain (e.g., life science) or discipline (e.g., psychology) specific.

Another critical concept to master as early in your undergraduate career as possible is the variety of ways in which the vast archive of academic knowledge is stored, organized, and accessed. For example, when you consider what constitutes all knowledge of biology, realize that although much of that information is found in books, including textbooks, there also exists a large repository that contains the long history of individual reports and papers, describing specific experiments and studies, which comprise the conceptual elements of biological knowledge. These individual publications are analogous to atoms that make up a solid structure. The knowledge of biology is the collection of individual contributions by a vast number of biologists from many countries working over the entire history of the science. Each contribution is part of the overall collection of knowledge that defines what is known in a given field or discipline.

Your campus library purchases access to that invaluable repository of information. These materials are not widely available on the "open web" through a Google search. When you are asked to find scholarly articles to use as sources for your first college paper, this is the kind of material you are looking for. You will use an article database licensed by the library to conduct your search. A librarian can help you identify the best database for your search and help you to search effectively.

The *journals* in which these papers are published tend to be highly specialized. For example, some journals in biology cover only research on biochemistry, heart physiology, or evolution. Getting a good understanding for how this information is organized and how it can be accessed is essential, especially once you select a major and begin to develop your own expertise in a specialized area. Again, librarians, subject guides, online tutorials, and even miniclasses presented through the library can help you learn to get the most out of your campus library. Learn to use this important tool as soon as possible; do not wait until there is a need for that knowledge.

Although much of the information that was available in the past in card catalogs and printed materials has been translated into electronic storage, there remain some resources in your campus library that require use of specialized equipment. For example, campus libraries may still have information stored on microfilm, often held in special rooms within the library. Likewise, many campus libraries have rooms that enable you to view and listen to visual and auditory recordings; not all knowledge is formatted as written words.

Two especially valuable resources to be familiar with as early as possible are the inter-library loan and course reserve services. The former enables you to borrow materials from libraries other than your campus library. For example, there may be a particular book that you need but your campus library does not have a copy. One of your librarians might be able to locate a copy in a different library. Through interlibrary loan your campus library can borrow the book from the other library for you to use. Articles borrowed electronically may be available within a day of your request, whereas books may take several days. Don't be afraid to use interlibrary loan. The course reserve service is a good example of how closely campus libraries function in support of teaching and learning. Many of your teachers will identify learning materials (e.g., books, articles from journals) that are part of the content for their course. Rather than requiring you to buy these materials, reserve copies are often made available to borrow on a very short-term, temporary basis (e.g., two hours or a day), or may be posted online for you to access.

When you need to do research for a paper or project, the library's website is the best place to start. Because the library pays for access to many resources, access to most of those resources is limited to users affiliated with the institution (current faculty, staff, and students). Links on the library's website may be configured to allow you to log in with a university ID that verifies that you are a current student, so that you can access this content even when you are off campus. In addition to searchable article databases, e-journals and other licensed content, all library websites include some kind of online catalog where you can search for materials owned by the library. The catalog will tell you which books and other materials are owned by the library and where they are located.

The library website should also point you to different ways to get help. You can probably get help over the phone, maybe through an online chat service, in person by dropping by the reference desk, or by scheduling an appointment with a librarian. As you explore, don't be afraid to ask for help. A college or university library has a wide range of services and resources. Even experienced faculty members sometimes have to ask a librarian for help using a new resource. Asking for help is not a sign that you are not well prepared for college. Asking for help will ultimately save you time by ensuring you are using the right resource and using it correctly.

Fig 23.3

Campus libraries also have study rooms that you can reserve individually or as part of a study group. Check you library's policies for reserving quiet study rooms as soon as possible, and consider using one of these spaces as an intentional strategy to develop a disciplined approach to studying. Some students find it valuable to regard a study space as similar to a place of work. By going to a study room on a regular basis, not just the night before a test, you can begin to establish productive habits that promote academic engagement and success. Additional resources found in libraries include copy machines, computer labs, and a variety of specialized services that augment learning such as writing centers, digital media help services, and at some institutions, some specialized equipment to assist students with some visual and auditory disabilities. To find out which services and resources are available at your campus library, review the library website or ask a librarian.

QUESTIONS

1. What do you think the term *information literacy* means?

2. When is the last time you were in a public library? Why did you go?

3. When you wrote papers in the past (e.g., in high school) did you have to use the library? If yes, how did you use the library?

FIGURE CREDITS

Figure 23.1 : andrew_t8, "Library with Spoke Tables," https://pixabay.com/en/library-la-trobe-study-students-1400313/.
Figure 23.2: ShuaiGuo, "Working at Library Table," https://pixabay.com/en/beijing-library-black-and-white-1877354/.
Figure 23.3: jarmoluk, "In the Library Stacks," https://pixabay.com/en/library-book-reading-education-488681/.

CAMPUS RESOURCES

Imagine that for some reason, a good reason, you were unable to participate in your college's orientation program. You then arrive on campus and discover that you have a variety of questions and need assistance with several matters. Where would you go for the following?

- You need to drop a class and add another.

- You need to obtain a campus email account.

- You plan to apply to medical school and would like to take advantage of any support services on campus.

- You want to verify that the transfer credits you had sent from a different college you attended during the summer have been received and credited toward your record.

- You need to apply for a student loan or have questions about a scholarship you received.

- You want to learn about how you can study abroad during the spring semester.

- You are a first generation student and would like to learn what support services are available for you.

The above scenarios merely scratch the surface of the types of assistance you might need as you transition to college. Managing your transition can be a real challenge. It can be quite confusing at first, especially if you have no role models in the form of parents, grandparents, or siblings who themselves have experience with college. Even for students who have such role models, the transition period can be overwhelming.

Modern colleges and universities are elaborate, complicated organizations, and most students need help navigating the array of offices, departments, and services available. As true in life generally, there are great advantages to having someone who can provide guidance in learning about all of the resources and opportunities awaiting undergraduates.

> **STUDENT VOICES:**
>
> *Realizing all the resources and the opportunities on campus to do other things and learn about other things and get better exposure was something that benefited me.*

Most colleges and universities have a large range of services and staff designed to support your academic success throughout your college experience. Each institution has its own unique set of support mechanisms, but there is a common set of services found at most colleges and universities. Although this chapter describes the general nature of these student resources, the best place for you to begin to understand what support is available at your college or university is your institution's *bulletin* or *catalog*. Be aware that many institutions are abandoning the old hard copy (printed) format of the bulletin in favor of more user-friendly interactive versions in electronic format. Most of the information you need can be found on the institution's web site.

The resource guide below is organized in terms of four broad categories of support services: *Advising, Advocacy, Personal Support*, and *Learning Support*.

ADVISING

The term *advisor* is a general label for someone whose job it is to assist and guide various aspects of your college experience; you will discover that going to college is more than attending classes and doing homework. Perhaps the most important advisor is an *academic advisor*. These individuals meet with you to explain curricular requirements and help you choose and enroll in classes. Academic advisors also assist you in making changes to your class registration and class schedule, and they help you explore and enroll in majors, minors, and certificate programs.

Academic advisors are well trained in the rules and regulations regarding the curriculum, and they are prepared to point you in the right direction for help with any issue, problem, or question you might have about your college experience. Often certain advisors work with particular kinds of students. For example, some advisors only work with students who do not declare a major when they first enroll in college, or with students who transfer from another institution.

Fig 24.1

FACULTY VOICES:

Even if an advising meeting is not mandatory, make sure to meet with your advisor.

Some academic advisors have faculty status. These advisors are usually associated with specific academic departments and advise students who have declared a major, as well as teach courses within the major. Professional advisors, in contrast, do not have faculty status; their only responsibility is academic advising. Both faculty and professional advisors may be affiliated with a department, a college within a large university, or an academic program. The latter are often referred to as program support advisors and are assigned to programs designed to meet the special needs of, for example, first-generation students, veterans, underserved minorities, international students, or honors students. In addition to guidance, these advisors often provide counseling, career information, and tutoring.

Another kind of advisor is a career advisor, who helps undergraduates prepare for postgraduate programs, jobs, and careers. For instance, it is common to find specialized advisors for students planning to apply to medical or law school (premed & prelaw students). Some career advisors are affiliated with career centers and provide guidance and support for students seeking employment after graduation. They can assist students in finding internships, service learning programs, and volunteer opportunities. Career advisors can also help you select a major that aligns with a particular career or job. They offer a variety of career counseling services including tests and surveys designed to help students choose a career path.

FACULTY VOICES:

Frequently visit your career center, which offers you rich resources, such as job interviews, internship and job opportunity listings, and help with resume and cover letter writing.

Finally, a category of advising that is growing in popularity involves helping you learn about and participate in specialized educational enrichment programming. For example, many students want to spend a semester or a year in an education abroad program, which enables you to complete course work at a university outside of the US Participation in service learning is another form of academic enrichment. It entails classes with hands-on experience in a work or service setting off campus. Some students may take classes that include spending time volunteering for a nonprofit organization in the community. Likewise, undergraduate research, which consists of opportunities to earn academic credit for research projects under the mentorship of a faculty member, is usually assigned to specific program advisors, especially at large universities. Majors such as psychology, chemistry, biology, and many others, now feature undergraduate research as a valuable component of their majors, and specific advisors in each department are available to help you take advantage of these enriching academic experiences.

Fig 24.2

ADVOCACY

Having an advocate, someone who has your back and works for your benefit, is an asset in many situations. Given the complexity of the college experience, it is important for you to be aware of the kinds of advocates available to assist you with issues you may confront as an undergraduate. Some of them offer advocacy merely as an extension of their normal roles. For example, you can think of your instructors and any faculty you work with as advocates. To this end, it is strategically valuable to get to know all of your instructors as early as possible in the semester. Go to their office hours, even if it is just to introduce yourself and have a brief casual conversation. Recognize that you are building relationships throughout your college career. Many of these relationships offer you personal resources that can help your academic success. Do not hesitate to seek guidance from your instructors and advisors for any question or problem you confront.

Beyond faculty and advisors, there are a number of offices and individuals that offer varying kinds of advocacy. For example, most of the classes you take will be administered through academic departments (e.g., Department of Physiology or Department of History). Each academic department has individuals who are expected to provide some advocacy for students. The chair of the department is one such advocate. Many departments also assign a faculty member as a director of undergraduate studies, which is a position that provides advocacy for students within specific majors. On the college level, the college dean and associate deans serve as advocates. Under some circumstances a provost or chancellor may serve as an advocate for you. You may face some problems and issues, for example, disputes between you and a faculty member or dean, that cannot be resolved to your satisfaction by others, in which case you may need to go see a provost or chancellor for advocacy. Get to know who they are, where they are located, and how you can contact them.

Another very important academic advocate found at most large universities is the academic ombudsperson. This individual is assigned the responsibility of helping students mediate academic issues, especially those that involve disputes between instructors and students. For example, you might disagree with a course grade or an action an instructor has taken regarding your performance in their class. The academic ombudsperson affords you a resource for appealing such actions and for resolving disagreements pertaining to a class or other academic activity. We recommend that you begin with an ombudsperson before seeking the help of, say, a provost or dean.

There are also specialized advocates who focus on issues like governmental and institutional regulations regarding disabilities, civil rights, social justice, and violations of student health and well-being. As an example, many institutions have established offices with advocates for students who have suffered discrimination, abuse, or even violence on their campus. Again, get to know the advocacy offices available to you at your specific college or university and know how to contact them.

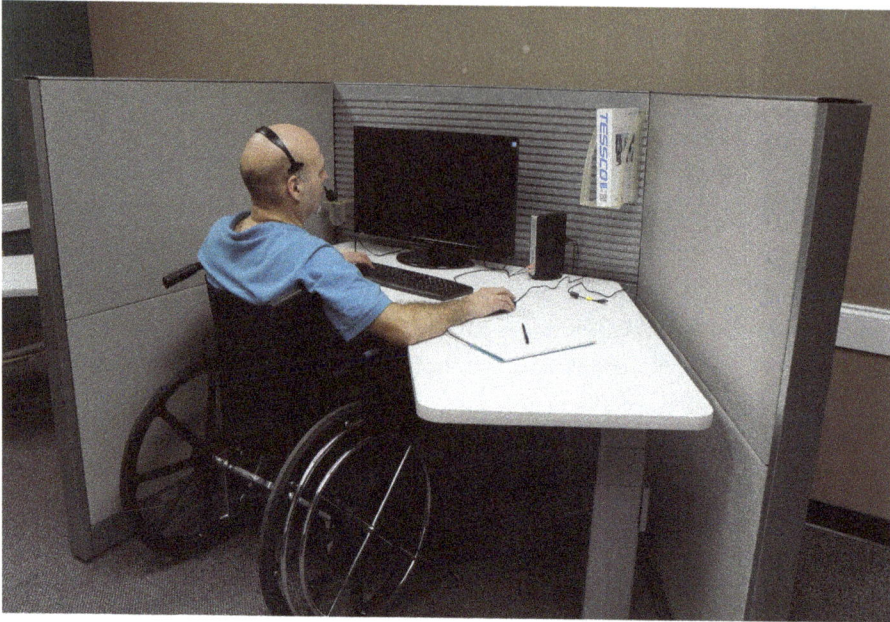

Fig 24.3

PERSONAL SUPPORT SERVICES

There are a number of campus professionals who administer services that support your academic success in ways that do not directly involve teaching and learning. Some of these services are essential components of your college experience. For example, most colleges and universities have a registrar's office. This resource provides assistance with your admission to the institution as well as your registration in classes. Usually the registrar's office is where you find information regarding your transcript. Other offices provide information and services related to financial aid, scholarships, and student loans. These offices are usually staffed with professionals who can not only process your requests and manage your needs, but also can offer counseling and guidance within their specializations. Some of the most fundamental needs of college students today pertain to financial issues.

Another important source of support at residential colleges and universities are professionals who manage residential life. These individuals are responsible for helping students with all aspects of living on a campus, including guidance on rules, regulations, and expectations of life in a residence hall. Large universities usually have a number of different people available to help you in each residence hall, but there are also professionals with more overarching questions and issues in a housing office.

Finally, two of the most important resources for students are medical care and personal counseling. Each college and university structures these services differently, but it is common practice these days to provide students with a broad range of support services to help manage health and psychological issues. Mental health counselors are well-trained professionals available to help with any personal issues related to your mental and emotional well-being, regardless of whether they are related

Fig 24.4

to academics or not. There is often a distinct counseling center on campus at larger institutions, but services are also sometimes available through student health offices. Given the degree to which general health contributes to academic success, medical and counseling services are particularly valuable. Know where to go if you feel ill for whatever reason; an unhealthy body cannot support a healthy mind. The stresses of the modern world can be compounded by the stresses of trying to succeed as a college student. You should always be ready to avail yourself of any and all support when needed, and it is imperative that you recognize when such needs exist.

It is important to emphasize that not all campus resources serve to help with problems. Successful students engage in a range of valuable activities outside of studying and going to class. *Extracurricular* activities, such as physical activities are an essential component of the modern college experience. Most universities have extensive physical recreational resources, from swimming pools and basketball courts to exercise rooms and bowling alleys. Most campuses also provide entertainment options like movie theaters and music venues. Perhaps even more important are the vast number of clubs and organizations that permit you to engage in productive social interactions that supplement and expand your curricular experience as a student. The options are usually easy to find on the college's website or bulletin. Many institutions offer information sessions about student organizations at the beginning of each academic semester. Learn what is available at your school and get involved. Being a good college student involves more than grades. You are preparing yourself for life, and you can enhance much of that preparation by developing your social skills and building strong connections with others.

LEARNING SUPPORT SERVICES

Learning at the college level is a much more complicated and challenging task than what many students, but not all (e.g., veterans), have experienced before. Accordingly, colleges and universities have created a variety of resources to enhance, supplement, and support, student learning. Some of these resources target specific kinds of support. For example, a writing center can help with specific writing assignments and offers general help to improve your writing. Likewise, digital media centers can help you use modern communication technologies effectively, again, both for specific assignments as well as general skill development. Many institutions have professionals available to help you create effective public presentations that rely on electronic media. Assistance with oral communication skills and use of basic information technology (e.g., support using a college email system) is also typically available on campus. These kinds of support services usually provide drop-in service, but many also offer short classes and online tutorials that are usually free to students.

In terms of assisted learning linked to classes, many institutions now arrange tutoring for various topics, such as math, psychology, and chemistry. In some cases tutoring services are housed in a common location, but some tutoring is administered through departments or residence halls. A popular strategy is to rely on *peer tutors*, who are usually upper level students who have done well in the course for which they serve as a tutor. There are also specialized tutoring services linked to certain student groups and programs at large universities, like student–athletes at large universities.

QUESTIONS

1. What is the difference between an advocate and an advisor?

2. How could a director of undergraduate studies help you?

FIGURE CREDITS

Figure 24.1: Free-Photos, "Two People in Office," https://pixabay.com/en/office-two-people-business-team-1209640/.
Figure 24.2: 27707, "Passport," https://pixabay.com/en/american-flag-usa-symbol-national-878059/.
Figure 24.3: dickusvi, "Disabled Student," https://pixabay.com/en/disabled-veteran-call-center-2199122/.
Figure 24.4: bastiaan, "Register," https://pixabay.com/en/register-keyboard-257986/.

INDEX

www.ingramcontent.com/pod-product-compliance
Lightning Source LLC
Chambersburg PA
CBHW080423270326
41929CB00018B/3143